COLOUR MEDITATIONS

D1041986

COLOUR MEDITATIONS

With Guide to Colour-Healing

*A Course of Instructions and Exercises in Developing
Colour Consciousness*

By
S. G. J. OUSELEY

L. N. FOWLER & CO. LTD.
1201–1203 HIGH ROAD, CHADWELL HEATH,
ROMFORD, ESSEX RM6 4DH

© S. J. G. Ouseley, 1949

FIRST EDITION, JULY 1949
FIRST IMPRESSION, DECEMBER 1951
SECOND IMPRESSION, DECEMBER 1954
THIRD IMPRESSION, MARCH 1957
FOURTH IMPRESSION, JANUARY 1960
FIFTH IMPRESSION, JANUARY 1963
SIXTH IMPRESSION, MARCH 1966
SEVENTH IMPRESSION, JULY 1968
EIGHTH IMPRESSION, JULY 1969
NINTH IMPRESSION, MARCH 1971
TENTH IMPRESSION, JUNE 1972
ELEVENTH IMPRESSION, JUNE 1974
TWELFTH IMPRESSION, MAY 1976

8524 3062 0

Printed in Great Britain by
Lowe & Brydone Printers Limited, Thetford, Norfolk

CONTENTS

PART I

PART II. GUIDE TO COLOUR-HEALING

CHAPTER I

THE POWER OF COLOUR

MANY people have quite definite ideas and feelings about Colour. The love of colour springs from the individual's inner consciousness.

Some people are far more sensitive to colour than others ; whilst some are attracted, even fascinated and thrilled by certain colours others are repelled or seem quite unaffected by these same vibrations.

It is quite apparent that Colour exerts a powerful influence on the minds and emotions. Colour is not a lifeless, static phenomenon, as many people ignorantly suppose, but is in reality a vital force, a strong power and influence in our lives. The starting-off question is naturally—What is Colour ? What exactly do we mean by it and why bother to study it ?

Science tells us that what we call Colour is a mode of vibration of light, and that all matter radiates light. All matter is luminiferous and therefore has a colour vibration. It is of vital importance to realise that matter is continuously emitting rays, and throwing off vibrations that materially affect us.

Light is defined as luminous radiant energy. The Science of Colour is based on the fact that matter and light are fundamentally inseparable and that when solid matter is reduced to its essence it becomes converted into a radiation identical with light. Thus light and matter have a twin affinity with each other.

This interesting fact of modern science is in line with the teaching of the ancient occultists who maintained that the Universe evolved from the primal Cosmic Fire, or Great

7

White Light which is an emanation of the Divine Being—the source of all light.

The Bhagavad Gita speaks of the *Imperishable Light*. "Behold the Form of me various in kind, various in Colours." God according to the Hindu Sages is the " Shining One."

According to Occult Science the White Light of Spirit breaks forth from the Third Logos, the manifested divine mind, in the form of Seven Rays, the seven spirits of light, and each Ray has its subordinate rays. Controlling the Seven Major Rays are the colour elementals (vibratory intelligences, spirits).

So much for the transcendental aspect concerning Colour. The Science of Colour has various aspects and applications. There is the medical or healing aspect, comprising Colour Treatment and Ray Therapy, there is the psychological aspect, the study of the influence of Colour on the mind and emotions, there is the esoteric aspect, the symbology and attributes of colours, and the colour aspects of the aura.

The Science of Colour is really part of the Science of Mind—Colour is basically a mental conception. Each Colour and sub-colour has a power and symbology entirely its own. We come across obscure allusions now and again in ancient literature to a Science of Colours. For example, in Ancient Egypt certain sacred manuscripts were written in colours—only the priests knew the true significance of the esoteric symbology.

The aim of Esoteric Colour Science is to build into the aura the seven pure rays—the seven jewels of the Yogi—so that the body, soul and spirit become revitalised, healed of defects and infirmities, transformed and inspired from *within*.

In studying Colour we are immediately struck by the fact that the mystic Number Seven crops up at the outset—the Seven Rays. The Science of Colour is based on the

" Seven " no less than the nature of Man—the sevenfold constitution.

Each Colour has seven aspects. Each Colour vitalises and animates, each colour heals, enlightens, supplies, inspires and fulfils. Take for example, the Red Ray—the Life Ray. Fundamentally it influences the physical body, but it acts on the astral, mental and spiritual bodies as well.

Red vitalises, with the element of life, all living matter. It is a positive magnetic vibration, the first ray of manifested being. The body deprived of the Red Ray becomes lifeless. Red is a powerful healing agent in diseases of the blood and circulation, debility and depression. Certain vibrations of Red act on the subconscious mind arousing the primary instincts and desires, and the same Ray supplies us with Life-force, energy, strength and physical power. Red also inspires heroic qualities—courage, love, adventure, enthusiasm—the Pioneer spirit.

The Red Ray seen in the Aura reveals the qualities of ambition, leadership, sociableness and generosity. The fulfilment or completion of the Red Ray influence is the man of action, courage and optimism.

At the other end of the colour-scale is the quieter, more elusive colour of Amethyst—the purest vibration of the Violet Ray. Amethyst belongs to the purple-violet group. Amethyst is the ray of spiritual mastery. In contrast to Red it influences the highest centre in man, the crown chakram or pituitary gland at the top of the head.

Amethyst vitalises man's spiritual nature with life-giving power and animates and expands the soul consciousness. It is a positive magnetic vibration but not physical. The soul devoid of the Amethyst or Violet Ray becomes dry and barren.

Violet, with its cognate colour Purple, is a powerful healing agent with a direct influence on the brain and nerves. It is stimulating to the spiritual nature and a strong purifying force. It is a specific in cases of sleeplessness as the physical senses succumb quickly to its influences. By acting on the pituitary gland Amethyst stimulates the intuitive centre of spiritual perception. A violet light is a great help in meditation and concentration of a spiritual nature. Wagner had violet draperies and materials about him when composing or creating music of the highest spiritual quality.

The Amethyst Ray supplies nourishment for all those cells in the upper brain that expand the horizon of our Divine Understanding.

Violet inspires the highest ideals in man as, for example, great works of art, music, poetry, prose and so on. It stimulates the desire to benefit humanity. The amethyst colour appearing in the aura reveals the presence of idealism, pure mysticism and spiritual qualities in the subject. The fulfilment or completion of the Violet Ray is seen in the great prophet, poet, musician, seer, the inspired mystic and teacher.

In the middle of the shining spectrum of Colour is the Green Ray—the key-note of our planet and the Colour of nature. The green radiance is essential to our health and happiness. It is the colour of balance and harmony. The Indian mystics speak of it as the ray that counterbalances cause and effect.

The Green Ray influences the heart-centre, affecting the blood pressure, and psychologically it influences the emotional nature. Green vitalises and restores the blood and nerves with nature's magnetism. The green-vibration heals heart disorders, emotional complexes and soothes the nerves of the head. A calm green light is an excellent remedy for headache. It is beneficial to absorb as much green as possible by using green lamps, green garments, green decorations in the house and by eating green vegetables.

Green opens and enlightens the mind and spirit with

Wisdom (the Yellow Ray) and Truth (Blue), which are the components of green. The colour is rich in the emerald life-prana, the inexhaustible energy of nature. Green inspires harmony and peace on the inner or subjective plane, and attracts success and progress on the outer or objective plane. Colour-vibrations have both subjective and objective aspects, the subjective influencing our inner mind and senses, and the objective aspect having an effect on our outer life and personality. The fulfilment or completion of the Green Ray in its subjective aspect is the man of balanced mind, the Man of Peace and Harmony, Sympathy and Generosity. The life of Christ shows many of the beautiful qualities and emanations of the Green Ray.

These three examples serve to show how the Rays act and the power and influence they pour out. The higher or super-physical Rays are actually emanations of the Great White Light of the Eternal Being. These great colour-vibrations are streams of force each one having a particular as well as a general function and purpose. Colour is thus a sevenfold force branching out into numerous channels and currents. Every human being incarnates under a particular ray and is influenced by other subordinate rays. The focal point of these rays and vibrations in man is in the Aura, the radiation of light which surrounds all creatures. The subject of the Aura is dealt with in a separate book.*

Your Aura is the key to your real self : it is the visible expression of your mind, soul and spirit—your powers, capabilities, aspirations, tendencies and potentialities. It also presents a reflection of your health condition. Upon the condition of your aura depends whether your personality is radiant, vital and positive, whether you are a source of inspiration and healing to others, whether you are expressing the light within.

* *Science of the Aura*, by S. G. J. Ouseley (Fowler & Co.).

CHAPTER II

THE SCIENCE OF COSMIC COLOUR

In no branch of Science will the serious student find more to interest and instruct himself and others than in the study of Colour and its relation to life.

In the truest sense of the word *Colour* is life. The splendid symphony of colour which we see manifested on all sides of the Universe is the visible expression of Divine Mind. It is the cosmic manifestation of the One Life Principle in the form of Light-waves.

All light is an emanation from the sun and colour is a mode of differentiation of this primal light according to the rate of vibration.

Occult science teaches that the visible universe as a whole, as well as each separate or organic part manifests on the physical plane through Cosmic Force.

In this Cosmic Force there are light-rays of a much higher order and power than these reflections, the colours with which we are familiar. Colour is the very soul of the Universe. According to Paracelsus and other great Masters of the secret wisdom, when a universal life-cycle begins it first appears as a rapidly vibrating mass of scintillatory colours—an infinite spiral of colours. Within the spiral globe resides the mighty cosmic power of transmuting spiritual energy into physical substance and vice versa.

The great ocean of light is radiated from the central sun, the storehouse of all energies and potencies, and the source of all life and light, warmth and motion on this planet. From this fact we can well appreciate the tremendous energy stored up in light and radiation in terms of colour. In studying colour we are studying a cosmic force of immeasurable and infinite power. We shall see later that Colour enters or rather pervades life on all planes of consciousness.

The ancient Egyptians were conscious of the power and influence of Colour and in their great temples and Wisdom Schools such as Karnak and Thebes, certain parts of the buildings were set aside as Colour-halls where the effects of colour vibrations were minutely studied and applied.

The ancient Egyptian priests, the inheritors and keepers of the esoteric wisdom of a vanished epoch left manuscripts showing their system of Colour-science which strikes us as a very excellent one. They applied the law of correspondence between the sevenfold nature of man and the sevenfold division of the solar spectrum.

The masses were not taught the full esoteric doctrine of Light and Colour, but were given only as much as they could assimilate. Thus, the Temple Masters taught, thousands of years ago, that the primary colours red, yellow, and blue, corresponded to the body, soul (mind) and spirit of man. This is a good rough classification of colours and has never been discarded although it has been enlarged upon. That the priests of the great teaching temples knew the full occult meaning of Colours is exemplified by the interesting philosophic poem—*The Vision of Hermes*.

The Indian and Chinese Mystic scientists also had a knowledge of Colour in their secret doctrine.

Although expressed in different ways and sometimes under a variety of symbols, the occultists of the past had broadly the same basis of colour-wisdom as we have today. The science of colour rests on the laws of light as manifested in the Seven Major Vibratory Rays. The Colour Rays are intrinsically related to the seven planes of manifestation and also to the Seven Major glandular centres in the human body.

Just as there is an esoteric (inner) and exoteric (outer)

meaning to all the phenomena of nature, so there is an esoteric meaning to the outward and visible rays of light comprising the spectrum. Ordinarily speaking, the sun is known
to radiate white light-waves capable of being resolved into
seven main constituent parts of different wave-lengths.

From the esoteric angle, however, the White light
(Spiritual sun) enters the consciousness of the soul through
the Aura and is diffused into its seven component colours,
each one infusing the appropriate soul-centre with power
and vitality.

In the ordinary sense, the Seven Major Rays are known
as :—

1. Red
2. Orange
3. Yellow
4. Green   } The Seven Rays of Life and Evolution
5. Blue
6. Indigo
7. Violet

These seven Major Rays signify a great deal more than
vibratory waves of light. Concisely speaking, the spectrum
is an epitome of the evolution of our Universe. Each of the
seven rays stands for one of the great evolutionary periods.

The Seven Rays are a manifestation of the seven great
Cosmic periods. The great Spiritual Intelligence known as
the Lords of Light who guide these evolutions are also called
the Spirits of the Seven Rays.

In reality the Rays are forces of infinite power and purpose emanating from the Supreme Source, the great White
Light, and guided and directed by all-powerful intelligences.
The Rays reach into our Souls. The word *Soul* is derived
from Sol (Sun) meaning the Light-centre within our being
as sparks from a Flame of the same nature, and are able to
be developed into flames also. In the Spirits of the Rays

are centred all the potentialities of the Highest dynamic powers and faculties.

The seven Cosmic periods are the conditions through which the Universe as a whole has passed, is passing or will pass in the future. This applies as well to the individual souls incarnating in various periods.

Occultism teaches that the Supreme Creator originally filled space at the beginning of Manifestation with His Aura, permeating every atom of the Cosmos with the Life Force. Thus from the Divine Aura radiated the Primal Light which the Supreme Being chose to be His Vehicle and Creative Power.

The whole planet—the oceans, the earth, everything we see manifested as mineral, plant, animal, and human forms —is dependent upon Light and its amazing properties and radiations for its very existence.

Not only the physical world—our material earth plane— but the higher worlds constituting our Universe—the etheric, astral, mental and spiritual planes—depend upon the same source of Light and have each a different rate of vibration.

Referring again to the seven Major Rays, Red, Orange, Yellow, Green, Blue, Indigo, Violet, the Occultist sees in them an ascending scale in the progress of evolution.

The first three periods corresponding to the Red, Orange, Yellow Rays, have already been passed through. We are now in the fourth or Green Ray Epoch, midway between the lower periods of struggle and bitter experience and the higher periods of soul-growth and spiritual faculties.

The Cosmic Wisdom teaches us that we have now reached the nadir of materiality—the outlook of the future is an upward advance into the higher vibration of the Blue Ray, and then an advance slowly towards the finer and more ethereal conditions of the Indigo and Violet Rays until the great septenary Ray of Manifestation comes to an end.

COLOUR BREATHING

Colour breathing is the realisation that the Universal Colour rays are in constant radiation from the sun, the planets, the earth, the ether, etc.

Students of Colour Science are exhorted to practise breathing with mental concentration on the beneficent rays contained in the universal spectrum. They should be consciously inhaled so that the whole being and the physical, astral, mental and spiritual nature, is diffused with them.

The appropriate affirmation connected with each individual colour should be repeated mentally during the breathing.

The Colour Breathing exercise is an invaluable aid in extending the consciousness and sensitising the soul-faculties. The diligent student will reap great gain in the form of inner peacefulness, physical and mental refreshment and improved general health.

The method is quite simple and should always precede each lesson in Colour Science.

Sit upright in a comfortable chair before an open window. Let the body slowly relax whilst you bend forward with the arms limp and exhale all air from your lungs. Then breathe in slowly as you gradually assume an upright posture, concentrating your mind on a point in the centre of the forehead. (This is the pituitary body which will be explained in a later lesson.)

Hold your breath as you count from one to twelve calmly and restfully—you will soon find that the counting becomes automatic and your mind is free to dwell on the new power, life, and harmony in the colours flooding your entire being.

Repeat the exercise several times. Later on you will be able to breathe deeply to an appropriate affirmation visualising the particular colours you desire to develop.

You will find that this exercise, when regularly carried out, replenishes your whole being with new life and also develops the power of seeing the Aura.

As Colour is a Divine Power it is, therefore, a vital force. It works through and in us, in every cell, nerve, gland and muscle ; and it shines in our Auras and radiates upon us from the atmosphere. In our higher bodies, Colour is an active power, exerting a tremendous influence on the mental consciousness, the soul and the spirit.

The value of a force such as Colour is that in essence it is spiritual. Strictly speaking, there is no need for any material equipment or appliances, although they are a useful aid in augmenting colour-treatments. The only essential requisite is a consciousness that is aline to Spiritual influences and a mind capable of concentration.

SUMMARY

(*To form the basis of Affirmations*)

1. Colour is a Vital Force. It is a manifestation of the Divine Mind. It is the original Cosmic vibration.
2. Colour is the Soul of the Universe. It radiates from the Central Sun like a great ocean of light. It is a force of immeasurable and infinite power.
3. The Seven Major Colour Rays fill space and permeate my soul and being. They are the manifestation of the Seven Great Cosmic periods. They correspond to the Seven Major glandular Centres in my body.
4. In the Spirit of the Rays exist all the potentialities of the Higher Being.

MEDITATIONS

Go into the Silence (that is shut out from the mental consciousness all material, astral and personal thoughts) and, being seated in a quiet room, repeat the following

Breathing Mantrum several times. Try to *feel* the affirmation within you.

Affirmations.

I am conscious of the Divine and Radiant Spirit of Love in my body, soul and mind.

O Spirit of Light, pour upon my mind thy sevenfold beam of brightness and illumination.

CHAPTER III

COLOUR IS A VITAL FORCE

SCIENTIFICALLY speaking, Colour is the result of etheric vibrations of different wave-lengths. Colour is not something merely static or ornamental but is active, vital radiation. Our very thoughts and feelings vibrate to Colour and our auras are throwing out bright or dull Colour-tones continuously. The power of Colour is so important a fact in our lives that modern medical science is showing an increasing interest in Colour-therapy—a subject, by the way, which the ancient Egyptians studied and practised !

The true significance of Colours and their influence on the health and personality is important to every man and woman.

Colour is a definite guide to temperament. When people state their favourite colours it is not the result of mere fancy or caprice, but a deep subconscious instinct that motivates them. This statement does not of course take into account the adoption of colours through external influences such as prevailing fashions, hair-dyeing and so on, but anyone taken unawares and questioned as to their colour preferences will give an answer illuminating to the expert. Not only will it throw a light on their psychological make-up but it will also indicate their probable talents— and their weaknesses. Some people respond far more deeply to colour-influence than others.

Let us commence with the three so-called primary colours Red, Yellow and Blue. These colours symbolise the body, soul (mind) and spirit respectively.

Red is essentially the physical colour : it is connected

with the element of fire, the essence of energy. The Red Ray controls the glandular centre in the body connected with the life-force and the vital functions. Red symbolises all the deepest of human passions—love, hatred, courage, revenge, etc. It is the colour of blood and has always stood as the symbol of warfare and naturally of brave deeds.

The varying shades of Red denote different qualities. Very dark, rich tones are often favoured by people of a somewhat close, selfish nature. The heavy shades usually appeal to the domineering, arrogant type of person as well as to those inclined to sensuality.

According to Colour-Psychology, the bright, clear reds are preferable to murky tones : scarlet, for example, denoting generosity and ambition. We invariably find all shades of Red associated with people who have strong forceful natures, people who *will* assert themselves and who abound in buoyant spirits and self-confidence. It is the colour of the extravert, the self-propagandist. Red denotes practicality and realism. Lovers of this colour are very often genial, active and vigorous people, but they are also capable of unkindness, obstinacy and lack of consideration.

People who are partial to Red usually have strong love-natures but more especially on the plane of the senses. Red vibrates in harmony with the senses and emotions and does not respond to the mind or reasoning faculties. Those for whom Red has a strong appeal will generally get on best with people who prefer violet, purple and golden shades.

Yellow denotes intellect, a love of mental employments and pleasures as opposed to the physical. It is an entirely different vibration from red. It usually appeals to people of intelligence and discernment. It has a stimulating effect in illness especially on the nerves : yellow controls the great glandular centre at the Solar Plexus. It is the colour of the Sun and is of a high vibrational rate : hence yellow-subjects are rapid thinkers and show great activity of mind.

Discrimination, tactfulness and cheerfulness vibrate to yellow.

It is a good colour for writers, artists and all creators, the paler shades are especially inspirational. Not all shades of yellow are good : certain shades, such as the dark mustard colours, stand for rather unpractical natures—people who dream the idle hours away and are lacking in character. Dark yellow is also associated with deceit and treachery.

The Orange Ray is one of the best of the yellow group. It is the colour of vitality, mental force and also of wisdom. This colour, however, has to be carefully used as few people can harmonise with its vibrations. Nervy people should never wear it.

Blue, both symbolically and medically, is the exact opposite of red. It symbolises harmony, calmness, courtesy and happiness. Blue is the colour from which the highest inspiration is born. Blue is not for the coarse, the sensual or the material-minded. It belongs to the ethereal, spiritual natures, the darker shades especially denoting refinement and " higher thought." Among the ancient Arabians saxe blue was considered efficacious in reviving lost love : whilst pale blue signifies simplicity, innocence and candour, electric blue great personal magnetism, deep blue, spirituality, and indigo is the colour of intuition and spiritual perception.

To despise the influence of colour in our lives is to show ignorance of the human temperament, so no intelligent person can afford to ignore individual preferences.

CHAPTER IV

COLOUR ATTRIBUTES

THE significance of Colours and symbols has long been the subject of research and enquiry. In the East various schools of esoteric knowledge concerning Colour have been in existence for centuries. In later days, the Theosophical writers have done much to promulgate the occult meanings of colour vibrations among the people of the West.

Modern science is also becoming Colour-conscious. Dr. George Crile of Cleveland, U.S.A., has demonstrated before The National Academy of Sciences that brain tissues emit visible colour radiations, infra-red radiation and also radiations of wave-lengths in and beyond the ultra-violet.

Colour, too, plays a large part in the human aura—the thoughts and emotions of a human being collect around the physical body in the form of fine vibrating waves or rays of colour.

There are seven major vibrating rays from which spring the seven basic types of human mentality and temperament; in addition there are several minor rays.

The seven Major rays are :—

1. Violet   Main characteristic—Spirituality
2. Indigo   ,,   ,,   —Intuition
3. Blue   ,,   ,,   —Religious Inspiration
4. Green   ,,   ,,   —Harmony and Sympathy
5. Yellow   ,,   ,,   —Intellect
6. Orange   ,,   ,,   —Energy
7. Red   ,,   ,,   —Life

Each of these seven major rays is divided into many sub-hues. The Violet Ray, for example, is subdivided into *Heliotrope, amethyst, orchid, royal purple, wistaria* and *lavender*.

As a general rule, clear bright Colours symbolise *good* qualities, whilst dark, cloudy, mottled shades denote *bad* qualities. Pale, misty, pastel tints signify the highest or ethereal states of consciousness.

In the human aura there are basic Colour-tones that reveal definite classes of talents, habits and character and there are numerous individual Colour-tones.

Occult science teaches that there is a correspondence between colours and the human constitution. Most readers will be aware that every human being thinks and feels on differing planes of consciousness and that he possesses a vehicle or mode of expression for each plane, viz.—the physical, astral mental and spiritual bodies. Each of these *bodies*, or forms of consciousness as they more correctly are, is related in some particular way to the three primary colours, *red, yellow* and *blue*, which symbolise respectively—

1. The Physical Body   (physical—etheric)
2. The Soul   (astral—mental)
3. The Spirit   (higher mental—Spiritual)

From this trinity emanate or evolve the secondary or complimentary colours—

> Orange
> Green
> Indigo
> Violet

From the foregoing principles it will be realised that there is a threefold aura which corresponds to the three-fold human constitution. There is the physical aura, the astral-mental aura and the spiritual aura.

RED. The symbol of Life, strength and vitality.

The Physical Nature. Clear, bright red shows generosity and ambition, also affection. An excess of red in the aura means strong physical propensities.

Dark Red, deep passion, e.g., love, courage, hatred, anger, etc.
The dark cloudy shades are evil and sinister.

Reddish-brown, sensuality, voluptuousness.

Very dark, rich tones, selfishness.

Cloudy red, greed and cruelty.

Crimson, lower passions and desires.

Scarlet, lust.

In contradistinction to these dark, earthy reds, there is the beautiful *rosy pink* the symbol of unselfish love.

Deep crimson shot with black, gross materialism.

ORANGE. The symbol of Energy.

The Etheric-Astral Nature.

Bright, clear orange, health and vitality.

Excess of orange in the aura indicates vital dynamic force.

Deep orange, pride.

Muddy, cloudy orange, low intellect.

YELLOW. The symbol of Mind and Intellect.

The Mental Plane.

Golden yellow, high soul-qualities.

Pale primrose yellow, great intellectual power.

An excess of yellow in the aura shows an abundance of mental power.

Dark, dingy yellow, jealousy and suspicion.

Dull, lifeless yellow, false optimism, visionary mentality.

Gold present in the aura is a good sign.

GREEN. The symbol of Harmony and Sympathy.

The Higher Mental Plane.

Bright clear greens bespeak good qualities.

Light green, prosperity, success.

Mid green, adaptability, versatility.

An excess of green in the aura denotes individualism, supply, independence.

Clear green, sympathy.

Dark green, deceit.

Olive green, treachery, double-nature.

The dark shades are the more sinister.

BLUE. The Symbol of Inspiration and Devotion.
The Spiritual nature.

Deep clear blue, pure religious feeling.

Pale ethereal blue, devotion to a noble ideal.

An excess of blue in the aura signifies an artistic, harmonious nature and spiritual understanding.

Bright blue, loyalty and sincerity.

INDIGO. Symbol of the Mystic Borderland.

Indigo, symbolises spiritual attainment and self-mastery—wisdom and saintliness.

VIOLET. The Symbol of Spirituality.

Deep purple, high spiritual attainment and holy love—the divine radiance.

Pale lilac and wistaria tints, cosmic consciousness and love for humanity.

Bluish-purple transcendent idealism.

MINOR COLOUR MEANINGS.

Light grey, fear.

Dark grey, conventionalism, formality.

Heavy, leaden grey, meanness, lack of imagination.

Greyish-green, deceit, duplicity.

Brownish-grey, depression.

Black, malice, vice, depravity.

Pink, modesty, gentleness, unselfishness.

Silver, versatility, vivacity, movement.

An excess of silver in the aura is a sign of inconstancy and a fickle nature.

Light brown, practical mind.

Dull, grey-brown, selfishness.

Clear brown, avarice.

CHAPTER V

THIRTY-ONE COLOUR MEDITATIONS

In the " Statement of Principles," issued by the Cosmic Colour Fellowship, the term Colour-Consciousness is defined as the " Soul's Awakening to the Divine Principle in the Universe—the foundation of true clairvoyance and intuition."

The author confidently believes that this object has been fulfilled in the following exercises in developing Colour-Consciousness.

The Aim of the Meditations is fourfold, viz. :—

1. To develop the spiritual faculty of Colour.
2. To develop the power of concentration.
3. To assist the student in applying the power of self-healing and overcoming negative conditions.
4. To create a telepathic link between all students of Colour Science.

The thirty-one Meditations form a miniature Course in training the Colour Faculty.

They should be rigidly followed throughout one month, allowing one per day. A quarter of an hour should be spent on each exercise. The best time is in the morning or just before retiring. It is essential to be quiet in mind and body ; adopt a relaxed position, seated in a comfortable chair or lying on a couch or bed, with either a dim light or a coloured lamp.

It is advisable to practise the Colour Breathing as explained in Lesson 1 of the Preliminary Course of Colour Science, issued by the Cosmic Colour Fellowship.

Go over each Meditation several times. The mental visualisation of the scenes set forth in the exercises may be found difficult for the first week or two, but on reaching the later stage you will be astonished at the thought-power you possess.

The main thing is to make your Meditations *radiant* and to see the Colours relating to the pictures in your mind.

By performing the exercises diligently and regularly for a month in the set order you will acquire the power of Colour-Consciousness and will possess a key to an illimitable Cosmic treasure.

Colour Meditations

Exercises in Colour Consciousness

Meditation 1.

Visualise a dark plantation of firs. In the background the setting sun, in a clear sky of soft finish, is sending gleaming rays over the white sheet of snow. The diffusion of Solar Colour melts radiantly upwards in Orange, Amber-Yellow and Green and finally tranquil Blue in the upper skies. Above the horizon a few small Golden clouds hang like a wreath—a crown of Cosmic Glory.

Realisation. At all times the Divine Radiance is sending forth the White Light of Spirit upon every being in the earth plane, in waves of Colour according to our individual needs. The Light shines through the darkness of matter dispersing the clouds of doubt, fear, and disharmony.

The Ray of Universal Love transmutes our weakness, Ignorance, Misery and engenders Vitality, Radiance, Wisdom and Peace. By absorbing the Effulgent Cosmic Rays we slowly transform our auras into centres of glory.

Meditation 2.

Picture mentally the refreshing Greenness of a meadow of young grass after a shower of rain. It gleams like a new carpet of Emerald velvet—bright, soft, tender. Above, the blue morning sky is fringed with flushed clouds—a cosmic harmony of ethereal Turquoise and Rosy-gold, blessing and glorifying the day.

Realisation. The trials, troubles and disappointments of life cannot separate the soul from the inexhaustible source of Goodness, Joy, Contentment and Harmony which are perpetually flowing upon it. The higher emanation must triumph over the lower.

When we are fully conscious of the Rays of Truth, Harmony, Beauty and Unity existing eternally in the Universe, our individual lives are changed—we are blessed and regenerated.

Meditation 3.

Visualise the evening sunshine falling over a quiet calm sea—the sun meets it so softly that no line of division is perceptible. From the darkening shore below comes the continuous plashing of the little waves breaking on the dim sand. Over the pale sea—in a sky where Purple turns to Rose and Rose to the molten steel and Sapphire colours of the coming night—the slim young Silver moon hangs in radiant clearness.

Swinging from her crescent, as by an invisible thread, is a scintillating jewel—a tiny, brilliant Star.

Realisation. The Golden Radiance of the higher spheres shines upon our souls at all times and floods our being with Life, Warmth, Power and Love without ceasing—yet, we are oftentimes forgetful and unaware of it.

Without the Cosmic Radiation, our own minds and thoughts are like little waves splashing helplessly in the darkness. When we are conscious of the Power, Love and Guidance which the Rays emanate we have no fear of the future—our way is a path of light.

Our life is illuminated by an Eternal Star that guides us perpetually.

Meditation 4.

Visualise a Red Camellia tree in full bloom, radiant with its deep Green glossy leaves, shining buds and vivid blossoms. Beneath it, a moss-walk leads through ilex and orange groves on sunlit terraces to a City of Gorgeous Colour surmounted by domes of tender Violet and Amethyst and fringed with pale Heliotrope and Citron.

The soft wind scatters the lovely Camellia blooms giving the ground a Crimson carpet or a drift like snow.

Realisation. The soul that is developing the inner consciousness of Colour stands alone, unfolding each Ray in silence and meditation. The student of Cosmic Colour knows that within himself is the gateway to the inner world of perpetual radiance. He trustingly treads the sunlit path of Golden Illumination and enters consciously the Temple of Absolute Light, leaving behind the outer veils of physical matter. When we stand naked before the inflowing Cosmic Radiance, every centre of our being is filled with new Life, Vitality, Courage, Peace, and Harmony.

We are transformed—like the earth with the colours of Spring.

Meditation 5.

Picture mentally the forms of great rocks jutting out into the sapphire-like sea, their bases washed by creamy foam and snowy spray. Far below lies a dark tunnel with deep Green water dashing through the opening. In its midst a narrow arch shows a brilliant glimpse of Light and distant sea.

Over the piled rocks cluster Orange lichens and above high water mark Purple thrift grows in every cranny.

Realisation. Our path in life is often strewn with difficulties, trials and burdens that seem gigantic and rock-like. We often seem in a dark tunnel, weighed down with grief and shut off from all Beauty, Joy, Freedom. Even Nature seems to lose her wonted glory.

When we give way to fears, doubts, thoughts of despair and depression we are losing ourselves deeper in the tunnel. By having faith and a positive attitude of mind, the most evil circumstances will be circumvented. In their very midst we behold the Archway of Light through which pours the splendour of the Seven Rays.

We receive Love, Strength, Power, Joy and Peace from the Eternal Source. When we become Colour-conscious, the Light is always shining in the darkness. Like the thrift we dwell above the troubled seas of life.

Meditation 6.

It is late afternoon in a great Gothic Cathedral. Gleams of mellow light are pouring richly across the dusky dimness and drifting in long rays past the noble pillars of warm stone through the ancient glass windows filled with jewel colours of Emerald and Ruby, Sapphire and Amethyst.

The organ-notes carry the thoughts through the dark aisles into a far world of rest and peace.

Realisation. Within our being is the jewelled Sanctuary of the spirit—the Cathedral of the Soul. It is our safe retreat in all times of stress, strain and anxiety. Peaceful is the atmosphere and beautiful is the Radiance of the Inner Sanctuary. The glory of the Seven Rays is enshrined here—the shining splendour of the White Light forever gleams within.

From the interior Altar of Colour we absorb the tranquil rays of Peace and Harmony, Joy and Life and we behold the luminous beauty of Truth, Goodness, Inspiration, Calmness and perfect Serenity. The Kingdom of Heavenly Colour is within you.

Meditation 7.

Picture a pergola against an azure afternoon sky—a regal

glory of Purple and Crimson. It is aflame with rambling roses and stars of Clematis in a jewelled setting of polished leaves. The burnished sun, sinking slowly on the golden horizon, throws an almost astral splendour on these divinely-wedded colours and bathes them in beauty of clearest light. And the world of hill and valley behind, Misty Blue and Amethystine, is shot across with long rays of Gold. It is nature's Altar of Colour.

Realisation. The Colour-conscious soul realises the perpetual splendour of creation. We are living in a Cosmic fairyland. When once understood the Divinity of which the Earth's light and Aura is an outward expression, we become in harmony with the Spirit of Life—the world is no longer a grey or barren place but a sparkling pageant of divinely-wedded Colour.

The trials and disappointments, the cares and vexations of life are all part of the same Golden pathway—though dark clouds reign for a time, the hills beyond are still Blue and Amethystine.

All fear, strain and doubt is an illusion, as grey and black are the negative aspects of Light and Colour.

Meditation 8.

Visualise a tall, pale-lilac pyramid-orchis, standing lonely and beautiful in the heart of a wood. Focused upon it is a great slanting ray of sunshine.

It points straight upwards to the effulgent Light that is pouring down. Round its base are grouped clusters of little red wild strawberries, looking gay with their three-fold leaves and clear White blossoms, like little children wonderstruck by the soaring height and beauty of a fairer influence. The huge solemn oaks look down like cosmic gods on this mimic world and above is the " height beyond all height."

Realisation. The Soul that is developing the inner

consciousness stands up like a spiral of light. The immediate result of developing Colour-awareness is that we discover our true identity. There blossoms within us a sense of increasing wisdom and illumination. We begin to realise that our Inner Self—our true being—is a focusing point of the great Cosmic Rays. We are linked by the forces of Light and Colour with the unchanging and the Eternal. We are reminded of the Presence of God in every Ray of Light and by every Vibration of Colour in Nature. From the Cosmic Soul radiates Infinite Power, Wisdom, Love and Intelligence.

Meditation 9.

Picture mentally a glorious sky of unbroken Blue. It is so clear that the eye seems to travel on into its depths to distance unending. The earth below is bathed in Sunlight—a world of Azure and Gold. In the foreground, the Ruby and Garnet leaves of a Virginia Creeper rise like flames in the clear atmosphere, throwing up long tendrils towards the Blue like an aspiring soul.

Realisation. Soul-growth and spiritual progress takes place when we transmute our Soul-colours by the Blue Ray—the calming and spiritualising radiation of the Cosmic Soul. Even on the physical plane we are reminded of the Rays of Truth and Beauty by the colourings of the sky and the garments of the earth.

The secret of joyful earth-life is to link consciously if possible with the Cosmic forces and powers. When we develop these powers in ourselves we can climb high and rise like flames with the celestial Aura. By right thinking and by valuing every aspect of life in its proper sense, we are able to extend our mind into the Superconscious Realm—the Eternal Fountain of Light. To achieve the higher consciousness it is necessary to rise above all resentment, envy and self-pity, above all complacency and selfishness, and above all hardness of heart.

Meditation 10.

See in your mind a beautiful assortment of roses in a quiet garden. They grow lightly and daintily at the end of the long stalks—some Cream and Yellow, shading to Orange and Apricot, some pale warm flesh-pink shading to deepest Crimson and Scarlet, with long buds like pointed flames. Their fair, bright heads glimmer like illuminated chalices against the rich vibrant Green of the Yew hedge. Their scent is full of the radiant memories of Golden Summer.

Realisation. Life is a harmonious progression like the evolving of a rose-bud into the glory of a rose. The cosmic forces are here at work transmuting and perfecting form and colour. The same forces work through and in our being. A life of ugliness, ill-health and disharmony is not the real life, but an empty parody of it. Karmic debts must be paid, but we must not allow our souls to become static and colourless we must develop our consciousness like a plant from seed to flower. The Colour Way is Beauty, Harmony and Peace. When we make contact with Cosmic Colour then the lower (dark) mind becomes healed of its blindness, discord and imperfections. We become like illuminated chalices filled with spiritual essences.

Meditation 11.

Picture mentally a border of deep Blue larkspurs—great spires of richest Ultramarine and Sapphire—gleaming in the radiance of an apricot sunset. The surrounding lawns are Golden Green in the beautiful clear light. Some Canterbury Bells, with transparent cups of pale pink, pure White and Violet-Purple, hold the vital sunshine until it seems to be burning and throbbing in their inmost hearts.

Over all hangs a peaceful atmosphere of stillness and calmness.

Realisation. Behind all the turmoil and unrest of material life, the Cosmic Soul dwells in radiant repose. You are part of the Cosmic Colour System. Nothing can disturb the serenity nor wreck the peace of the Colour-conscious mind. When you realise your affinity with the Universal Soul of Nature, you attract to yourself the Rays of Peace, Joy and Harmony, Health and Vitality, and you begin to know the meaning of radiant repose.

The vast display and majestic splendour of Colour in the kingdom of Nature is a faint reflection of the Eternal Radiance that is behind the sun, the stars and the flowers. By earnestly studying Cosmic Colour Science we daily advance towards this Perfection. Life becomes an illuminated pathway. We should constantly endeavour to live in the consciousness that we are creatures of Light, spiritual beings, Rays of Divinity, abiding continually in the Eternal Radiance.

Meditation 12.

Visualise clearly a quiet, mellow afternoon sky. Soft filmy clouds woven of purest dream-colours—faintest Rose and pure Gold—draw slowly, calmly to the West, across a background of pale and distant Blue, melting in clearest Green. No wind nor any sound, except the occasional hush and rustle of bird flights high up in the still air.

The last sunbeams slant along the smooth Green sward as the day sinks into the depths of Cosmic peace.

Realisation. Love and peace is ever to be found in the Soul of Nature. When we contact the Cosmic Soul we enter into the interior harmony of the Universe. We find the beauty and tranquillity of the Stars and the radiance of celestial colours within our own higher mind. Our soul extends and grows in health and wisdom, beauty and peace, in line with our spiritual unfoldment and proceeds with rhythmic harmony, like the pattern of Radiant Colour that crosses the heavens and is absorbed by the Cosmic Soul.

As we become at one with the Soul of the Universe so do harmony, order and peace manifest in our life—our thoughts become tinged in faintest Rose and purest Gold.

Meditation 13.

Picture in your mind a high, secluded hill, crowned with the restful green of clustering trees. It is peaceful and serene. Behind and above, wild clouds of grey and dark purple with silver rifts between them, hurry past on the swing of the wind—beautiful but stormy, ever changing like the changing things of the earth. Upright, changeless and steadfast stands the secluded hill—a Green symbol of the faithfulness which is the strength of love.

Realisation. The soul, attuned to the Cosmic Stillness, remains steadfast amidst the storms of life, surrounded by the eternally-peaceful Green Ray.

The power of the soothing Green Ray increases as we hold our mind on the Colour. Concentrate your thoughts upon the Green Hill and just relax. To attain the Cosmic Consciousness and realise perfect peace and ease of body and mind, we have first to become still; not still in the merely negative and passive sense, but still in the cosmic or spiritual sense. Not by denying any feeling of life and emotion but being inwardly still in the etheric, astral and mental bodies and relaxed by concentration on the Green Cosmic Vibration. This stillness is the radiant repose of the Infinite and Eternal and is in fact the highest possible state of mental and spiritual activity.

Meditation 14.

Visualise a peaceful sky of pale Lilac and Rose, hanging serene over the departing day. The surrounding woods are very quiet and self-absorbed as they await the silent descent of night.

The earth grows dusk, but the cosmic-flush of the heavens lingers, blessing the earth with a loving radiance of Pink and Opal—its token of remaining glory—like the burning thought of some divine joy that has gone.

Realisation. At numerous periods in our life, there comes the feeling of being forsaken, abandoned, lonely and forgotten. The warm Rose-radiance of Love seems to be withdrawn. Our souls seem left wide open to the coldness of indifference and neglect. Yet when we descend into the very depths of night and enter the darkness alone, we find God is there. When you feel forsaken concentrate on the Green Ray and the Cosmic Soul, with its warm cheering Radiance, will draw near to you. When we feel pressed down by difficulties and experiences too great for us, then we discover even when all seems hopeless, humanly speaking, that there is a Ray of Light shining perpetually upon us.

Over our heads there is always a sky of Lilac and Rose— if our earth-senses could but see.

Meditation 15.

Picture mentally some clustering bunches of Acacia bloom, swinging milk-white and sweet amid the pale Green leaves, high up against the Azure sky. Flower upon flower, like chains of beauty, as if it were from heaven to earth. Their ivory blossom and faint Green leaves frame tiny spaces of faintest light—Pearl and Amethyst—from a sky of drifting clouds and silver gleams.

Realisation. Love and beauty is the keynote of the Universe. The value of Colours is that they possess a power or vibration of their own that differs according to the quality and radiation. Thus positive or magnetic colours have the effect of awakening in our souls feelings and powers akin to themselves.

When feeling depressed or discouraged, anxious or depleted, you should visualise Red (Courage and strength), Green (hope and faith), Scarlet (Victory), Emerald (Joy), Bright Blue (Happiness), Yellow (Guidance and Wisdom), Amethyst (Spiritual Awareness). You will find that your inner soul—the real source of your thoughts and health— responds to the power and vibration of the Rays. Without the uplifting and inspiring influence of Colour our minds would be perpetually in a state of darkness and turmoil.

Meditation 16.

Visualise a standard rose-tree covered with large pink blooms. The pure Colour and exquisite shapes stand light and radiant, against the dark rich background of the great old trees. Nearby are two tall White lilies swaying in the breeze and shaking the fragrance from their bells. They look like White spirits conversing with one another, pale, slim and graceful.

Such perfection makes the whole world seem beautiful.

Realisation. Colour Realisation is an expansion of consciousness—a lifting of the veil of dull matter—and a recognition of the spiritual reality and divine principle throughout the Universe. The result of Colour Consciousness is that we discover our true identity. We develop a sense of increasing power and a widening perception ; we perceive the Light that permeates every substance, for the ultimate essence of matter is indestructible Light. By cultivating Colour Awareness in our lives and by contemplation of the beauty of Nature, we become transformed into the Divine Image and thus are able to see God, the Source of Light, everywhere. When the mind is filled with radiant thoughts and the aura aglow with Cosmic Colour then the Soul becomes impervious to dark and negative vibrations.

Radiant health and personal efficiency is the result.

Meditation 17.

Picture mentally an effulgence of Mauve and Turquoise —a deep, clear illimitable Azure sky. The earth below is warm and soft, decked with masses of Purple-flamed Lilac. Peach-coloured rhododendrons lift up great bunches of blossom, pale Wistaria hangs its sweet-scented clusters against a rose-coloured brick wall. All seem to mingle in Cosmic rapture with the Blue above until they become one living joy and harmony, peace and stillness.

Realisation. If we would know and enjoy inner peace and harmony and also live our life polarised to our particular Ray, we must learn the secret of inner stillness. Our auric colours must harmonise. To feel and experience the Cosmic Soul—life, we have to be still, to be quiet within, to withdraw from the maddening crowd. All Cosmic or esoteric teaching is of this nature ; it is only the external, the elementary, the material, that is noisy and restless.

The more outer noise and turmoil there is in our lives, the further we are removed from our centre of Light.

The way of the Spirit is not noise, excitement, and discord but quiet, calm irradiation.

Peace, Joy, Happiness, Health, Harmony and Beauty flow from the Cosmic Soul.

Meditation 18.

Visualise a hedge-bank in a leafy lane, full of bright summer colours. The grasses are tall, tremulous and vivid Green. The Speedwell has opened its Blue eyes and shines among the fallen petals of the overhanging wild-Cherry. Buttercups hold up their Golden discs and the hedge is crowned with its first White garland of hawthorn—delicate pink centred flowers and pearly buds.

There emanates a healing aura of harmony, love and sweet peace.

Realisation. It is necessary to spend a certain time every day in creating an inward awareness of union with the Cosmic Soul and in realising our oneness with the Eternal White Light as expressed through the varied Colour Rays of Love, Life, Joy, Peace and Wisdom.

This practice results in unity of life, in health, success and progress on all the planes. Meditation is the alchemy that transmutes the greyest thoughts into bright cosmic vibrations. The contemplation within the mind of Colour Rays first results in a new condition of thought and consciousness and afterwards manifests in outward affairs.

The peace of the Cosmic Soul is an interior order and harmony to which all true Colour-conscious minds have access at all times.

Meditation 19.

Picture mentally a stormy sea with the snowy spray dashing against the rocks as the incoming waves hurl themselves shorewards. Then, for one beautiful moment, a glorious rainbow spreads across the sky as the sunlight darts down from behind the dark, frowning clouds. A Green beam of light flashes in the water and discloses a radiant islet with White waves climbing up the steep sides of Amethyst-shadowed rock.

The clean, stormy wind blows wildly, and the fresh, delicious air is full of life and vitality.

Realisation. Like the immovable rock we are held in the One Universal Power—nothing can assail or disturb us. For there is only one Universal Spirit of Life—the Cosmic Soul which infuses our Auras with rainbow-hued Colour and spreads over our inner horizon like a stream of radiant harmony. The life of the Illumined Mind is a life of mastery and positive force. Negative vibrations have no power. We are surrounded by Infinite Cosmic Rays, by a plenitude of power and life, the emanations from the Universal Soul. From the Divine Centre, Source and Spirit of Infinite Light, Love, Wisdom, Power and Harmony, comes a reaction according to our need. Not only within our being but around us on all sides is the vast, inexhaustible Cosmic Soul—the only Power.

Meditation 20.

See in your mind a radiant sunset of flame-colours and Purple—the whole Western sky shot with every shade of Crimson and Gold and Amethyst.

Picture the sun sinking slowly down behind the rim of the world. The vast radiation stretches far out embracing everything and reaching toward the East where the sky is full of heavenly Turquoise. Every little cloud is flushed with purest Rose—the Cosmic Emblem of Divine Love.

Realisation. The Cosmic Colour student regularly visualises himself as surrounded with a Colour-aura or atmosphere entirely to his own liking. As often as possible, he wears his Ray Colour in some physical form of manifestation, and above all he is accustomed to seeing himself psychically enveloped in it ; by so doing he gains confidence in his ability to attract to himself whatever he desires and to surround himself in the aura of his choice.

Every colour (and sound) has a special signification and whether you can produce the tone or colour in your outward sphere or not, insist upon having it with you subjectively— by this means you make the cosmic atmosphere subservient to your needs and you are in a condition to extract from it whatever you please.

Meditation 21.

Imagine you are at the extreme North of Europe where

during the summer months there is no general darkness between the evening and the morning. Nevertheless at about ten in the evening the whole host of Colours, which belong to the setting sun, are displayed. From this hour onwards an unexpected and extraordinary change begins. There is an intensification of brilliant Orange and Yellow as well as of darkest Green and Blue. A stupendous drama takes place which approaches its height close to midnight. At this hour the sun and sky are nothing but shining Gold, forcing a pathway over the sea. Rocks and mountains rise black out of the dark water and even the clouds are like sombre curtains ready to be drawn across the glorious Cosmic Splendour of the Midnight Sun.

Realisation. Light and darkness exist in the Soul of every human being. But the soul that is polarised to Spirit knows no darkness and is never shut off from the Eternal Splendour of the Celestial Sun. Light is Spirit. But no human eye has beheld the Light itself. On the physical plane we can only study Light in connection with matter. It shines on objects and illumines them so that we can perceive them. And Light, in contacting matter, turns into Colour. As a direct manifestation of Nature, Light remains hidden from Man. We can only calculate its speed, propagation and its general effects. The real nature is unknown to material science. Cosmic light for instance, has a much greater velocity than 186,000 miles per second.

Its real velocity is instant presence.

Meditation 22.

Picture a sheltered bay, bounded on each side by low peaceful cliffs. The calm Green sea rolls tranquilly in towards flat weed-covered rocks and soft yellow sands. The waves break with a gentle monotonous song upon the shore. On the rich brown seaweed the curling waves splash in whitest foam. The grey-blue afternoon sky seems to hang low over the sea—the winds are asleep and all storms far from this inlet of peace.

Realisation. When the barque of our life sails lightly upon smooth summer seas, driven by the fair winds of health and prosperity ; when friends are plentiful and eager to help us ; when social favours and influence come to us to gratify our desires—then, indeed, the thought, " This world is good enough for me," seems true. But when we reach the end of the smiling sea of success ; when the winds of adversity have blown us upon hard rocky shores and the waves of suffering threaten to engulf us ; when friends fail—then we must look for guidance to the cosmic realms. When the mariner scans the sky in search of a guiding star, he finds the whole heavens in motion. To follow almost any one of the myriad of wandering stars would be to court disaster. The guiding star must be steadfast and immovable—there is only one such, namely, the North Star. By its guiding light the ship is brought to safety. By tuning-in to the right wave-length of our fixed Ray of Destiny we sail through tumultuous seas to the islet of peace.

Meditation 23.

Visualise a young cherry-tree in glorious dress of Carmine and Vermilion ; every long drooping narrow leaf glows with colour. It reigns over the orchard like a king in royal robes, for all the other trees, planted in rows that carry the eye down long fascinating vistas, are as yet Green or only slightly touched with Russet Red.

No wind stirs, the earth rests in perfect calm, and the Red leaves burn undimmed by the slight mist that rolls over the hills.

Realisation. The Cosmic Soul—the mind of the Infinite —supplies what is necessary at *the time* ; we have to trust the Source of all Life for the future. Neither must we cling to that which is given us. " Freely have ye received, freely give," is the Cosmic Law.

The Colour-conscious soul is " like a tree planted by the waters, that spreadeth out her roots by the river and shall not see when death cometh, but her leaf shall be Green."

We are rooted and centred in the One Light and Life from which everything springs.

Meditation 24.

Picture mentally a great beech-tree changing slowly to autumnal colouring. The leaves are burnished and shining with every shade of copper, Red-Brown and Gold. The straight, strong stem still retains its smooth gleam of mother-of-pearl and silver. The whole tree glistens like a gorgeous piece of jewelled nature-workmanship and the deep Blue sky, visible in spaces of divine colour between the leaves, is clear and bright and majestic.

Realisation. What is termed " realisation " is an expansion of consciousness in which we pass from effect (as experienced by meditation and reflection) to Cause, finding ourselves one with the Cosmic Essence or Divine Principle. This is what is meant by knowing the Truth. One of the main objects of the Cosmic Colour Fellowship is that men should know the Truth behind the familiar phenomena of Light and Colour. By practising Colour Meditation and developing Colour-awareness we contact the Light within us, and then greater Light and Understanding come to us. This is why sometimes beginners and preliminary students get wonderful results—they use the interior Light of Truth they possess.

Meditation 25.

Visualise a great, wide expanse of land and sky—from the vantage point of a high hill. Far below, the plain with its pale Green fields, rounded Blue-shadowed trees, and Purple woods stretches to the distant horizon where all is dim and soft. The sky is full and vibrant with pure light, Golden in the beams of summer afternoon. Little clouds gather in the West to meet the sinking sun, and the sweet wind blows over everything, thrilling the earth and heaven with its living breath.

Realisation. Time and space are merely limitations of human consciousness. It has been said that there is no place but the *presence of God.* This implies that as regards " place " we are in the real spiritual Universe or Infinite Life now, but we may be either in Heaven or Hell according to our state of consciousness and aspect of life. If we incline to darkness or blackness in mind, thoughts and feelings then we are in Hell most certainly ; if however we love the things of the Kingdom of Light and delight in pure Colour then we are most certainly in Heaven.

When we enter into the Cosmic Truth, every day the world is made new and life becomes more radiant and beautiful.

It is progressive like the colours in spring. Daily our life becomes more beautiful and harmonious.

Beauty—Joy—Harmony do not come from without but are qualities that radiate from within.

Meditation 26.

Picture mentally the earth lying veiled in the mystic sleep of night. A light diaphanous vapour wraps the wet grass and the silent trees, which seem like intangible brooding shadows. The Silver floating mist, like the aura of a spirit, is all woven through with White Moor Light, and high above the earth in her astral dream, hangs the Indigo sky, jewelled thickly with scintillating stars. No sound disturbs the breathless quietude but the rhythmic falling of dew from unseen leaves. The Cosmic beauty is almost too ethereal for mortal mind, but its balm sheds on the soul a radiant blessing beyond all words.

Realisation. At night the living creature feels itself drawn into the Earth and it sinks down upon it and the force of gravity embraces it mysteriously, the senses close themselves, but the Light that belongs to them remains in the consciousness like a hidden Sun. From within, this—our own Sun—shines into the night of the veiled senses, whilst from below the Earth—the Sun of the Midnight—exerts its celestial power upon us through the Earth's body. Just as the human organism during sleep re-establishes and builds up during the night its harmony of forces, so also the Earth-organism re-establishes at night the equilibrium of its cosmic forces upset during the day by the action of the Solar radiation.

Meditation 27.

Picture a majestic sky of striped Azure and White—light ribbons of cloud stretched across the pale Blue, delicately faint and far. Golden shafts from the setting sun glance through the darkening trees, the departing light casting a crown of glory on their tops and a glowing aura round all the outer leaves which change to Red-gold at its magic touch.

The sky is radiantly bright, and the distant woods, dusky against it, are full of suggestion and mystery, while these last rays of beauty linger like a divine memory of the day that is done.

Realisation. " God is Light "—the Light which became Life in man. It was dim and achromatically diffused in the early Atlantean Epoch, as Colourless as the atmosphere of a fog, but as man evolved so Light became refracted in multitudinous hues and was differently absorbed by each individual. Thus diversity manifested and mankind went through the mystic rainbow with its variegated and beautiful colours. The bow of the heavens may therefore be considered as a gateway to the " promised land "—the world as now constituted. The present brilliant display of Colour is a sign that the basis of the present age is segregation.

So many people live on the material plane cut off from the White Light of Spirit.

Meditation 28.

Visualise a fresh, seaweed-scented shore. The tide is far out and between land and sea stretches a great flat space of beautiful mingled colours—warm rocks, honey-tinted sand scattered with White and Purple shells and rich Golden-brown seaweed which encircle crystal-clear pools full of light and sky reflections.

Far off the waves are chanting, and the wild vibrant calls of many sea-birds fall like music through the windless air. A sky of dove-grey and opal broods over the bay—there is a feeling of Cosmic peace, which is at the same time infinite longing, radiating like a blessing over all.

Realisation. Many are the ways through which men pass from the lower to the higher. The Cosmic Soul may be found in many different ways and by diverse systems. For the Colour-Awakened Soul the most effective way is by cultivating the inner sense of Colour-consciousness. The practice of seeing the beautiful in everything leads to harmony and peace. As we meditate on the Seven Rays our souls float quietly out into the Cosmic. Then resting in the bliss and peace in which the Spirit of Light abides we breathe deeply of the Divine Breath.

Meditation 29.

Picture a sea of Bluebells seeming to flow over the woods —the waves of Sapphire light and Amethyst shade fill all the scene with beauty.

Above, the sky answers the lovely colour and the warmth, sweetness and fragrance bring a thrill that is almost unbearable in its poignant joy. Through the hanging wreaths of leaves which sway and quiver in the breeze, the clear unbroken Blue sky is caught and held like the radiant gleams of pure Colour in a cathedral window. The whole vision is a cosmic prayer—an offering of loving worship.

Realisation. Colour is one of the avenues that lead to Cosmic consciousness. The only thing that is real and eternal is Spiritual and this Spiritual Reality is Perfection in all its wonderful, beautiful and radiant forms. There is only one Reality and this is God and His Perfect Expression—the Cosmic Soul. This perfect Spiritual Universe is not " a city afar off " for the Kingdom of Heavenly Colour is in our midst. When our mind, thoughts are all in harmony with the great cosmic rays and if this condition of mind is extended to all our actions and our dealings with our fellow-men, then we are truly becoming Cosmic-minded.

Meditation 30.

See in your mind a glorious October carpet of newly fallen foliage. The brown earth is spread with a deep rich covering of warm russet and copper, crimson and red— thickly scattered leaves of all delightful shapes ; thrown down, here and there, in wonderful patterns on the subtle colours, are great fans of horse-chestnut Gold and Green.

Over the horizon is an exquisitely lovely sky melting into Amethyst-pink, like the tender bloom on a dove's breast, and changing in the higher regions, from Purple to radiant Azure.

Realisation. Through looking for the Colour and Beauty in life we are not only enabled to find it, but also, through realising the true nature of life we are led to co-operate with it instead of opposing it. The Cosmic way is harmonious, peaceful and beautiful. The Soul of the Cosmos emanates Love, Beauty, Harmony, Peace and Sympathy—and when we respond all is well.

On attaining Colour-consciousness we begin to see the Soul of Nature and to express the best, the richest and the highest in our lives. Remember that the vast powers and intelligence of the subconscious mind operate in conformity with the spiritual rays that illuminate the inner consciousness.

Meditation 31.

Picture a group of crocuses in early Spring. They are still folded buds but will soon open into bright cups to hold the sunshine. Best beloved of all the first spring flowers. Notice how their fairy-like Colours come so purely out of the brown earth.

Golden-yellow with tiny black stripes at the base of the petals, Amethyst and deep Purple restful to the soul, and delicate White, streaked with Violet, opening to show the red-gold stamens. They herald the blaze of Colour that the Spring is heir to. And when the days are cold and sunless, when the skies are grey and songs grow silent, the crocuses are there to tell of Beauty and Radiance.

Realisation. If, as a student of Colour, you have diligently performed the preceding thirty meditations, you have caused to stir deep down in your soul, a motion or vibration that is linked with the pulsating, vital Soul of the Universe. Just as the spring sunshine stimulates the seed in the dark earth and animates it into vigorous life, so also the Cosmic Soul will pour through your Aura the glorious Radiance of Divine Life, Health, Richness, Love and Harmony.

The Cosmic Rays flowing into your Soul are creative, illimitable, substantial and vital forces with tremendous powers and potentialities. They will enable you to draw to yourself the things that you desire—like the plants' growth; from the depths of their being they will supply you with perfect Health, Wisdom, Harmony. The Cosmic Rays are the primal creative and formative forces that caused the first manifestation of Light, Life and Being over the Solar and planetary substance itself, and which continue to radiate upon every living thing from their boundless, immeasurable and inexhaustible source. Each of the Seven principal rays is the embodiment of Divine Power, Purpose and Fulfilment.

CHAPTER VI

THE ADJUSTMENT OF LIFE THROUGH COLOUR

In this chapter we will show how to make practical use of Colour in rebuilding and restoring the harmony of life.

The student should first realise that Colour produces three main effects, viz., 1. Restful, 2. Re-vitalising, 3. Inspiring and stimulating.

A colour is restful when it produces a quiet and passive feeling, or a state of contemplation and reflection. One of the best colours for this is Green, the particular shade depending on the individual. A colour is re-vitalising when it can create conditions of change, balance, expansion, contentment and improvement.

Red and Green have this power.

Inspiration, Stimulation are qualities inherent in Colours which excite the feelings of hope, activity, aspiration, ambition, desire, or which cause liberation of thought and feeling through the consciousness of peace, joy, intuition, realisation and the soul's higher functioning.

This is the keynote of the Blue Ray.

Remember that the great trinity of colours, Red, Yellow, Blue, corresponds to the great natural divisions—physical, mental, and spiritual.

Colour being vibration expresses itself according to the different rates of vibration operating in a particular plane. Thus, the physical plane being of a low vibration and density attracts colours of a low vibrational rate, such as rich gelatinous Reds and certain heavy Orange tones. The Mental plane being of a higher vibration finds certain bright, shining, transparent colours such as pale yellow, most congenial to it. The spiritual plane which vibrates most rapidly finds affinity in colours of a very luminous, phosphorescent type of high-vibrational rate.

For greater clarity of understanding and using the rays of Colour, I will give a colour table embracing the three-fold divisions of life.

1. *Physical.*	2. *Mental.*	3. *Spiritual.*
Restful—	*Restful*—	*Restful*—
Green.	Indigo.	Moonlight Blue.
	Green.	
Re-vitalising—	*Re-vitalising*—	*Re-vitalising*—
Orange.	Royal Blue.	Gold.
	Èmerald Green.	Rose Pink.
{ *Inspiring*—	{ *Inspiring*—	{ *Inspiring*—
{ *Stimulating*—	{ *Stimulating*—	{ *Stimulating*—
Vermilion.	Yellow.	Amethyst.
Scarlet.	Violet.	Purple.
		Violet.

The above table is a concise key to employing Colour in restoring your nerves and rebuilding your health in body, mind and spirit.

Supposing, for example, that you are physically tired or exhausted, mentally fagged-out and overcome, and spiritually worried or depressed.

You can get rid of this condition by applying the correct Colour vibration either naturally by the use of a lamp emitting coloured rays, a coloured screen or drapery, or metaphysically by getting into contact with the cosmic colour currents flowing through your Aura.

The visualisation or consciousness of the Colour currents by mental awareness is the best method and all students are exhorted to concentrate their minds upon it until they have acquired the fullest power and skill.

Whatever technique is used, the student should never lose sight of the law that relates Colour with breath—the science of Colour is intimately connected with the science of breath.

Some of you may be aware that when you see certain colours you cannot resist drawing in a deep breath—You feel a desire to drink in that colour, and even to hold your breath as you behold it. These are the rest-giving colours. Other colours, the mental re-vitalisers, draw sudden exclamations of joy and wonder from you, whilst others have the effect of making you close your eyes and filling you with awe—in other words, raising your vibrations. These are the inspirational and stimulating colours.

These are not mystical or occult experiences, they are the normal reactions of colours on most people.

Suppose you were walking through the drab, leaden-coloured streets of an industrial city with its brown and grey buildings—suddenly you have a vision of the soft green and purple lights of the sea in midsummer. Would you not mentally drink in that colour and try to absorb it ? Green acts like a sedative, soothing the nerves and receiving the life-force.

It is very beneficial for the student to experiment with the effect of different colours. Begin by meditating on the colours of nature, noting carefully the results of your experimenting and tabulating them.

The country, the sky and the sea are full of natural colour-screens which you should consciously absorb. Make your mind as quiescent as possible and concentrate on the colour whose vibrations you desire to draw in to yourself—it is necessary to be perfectly relaxed, physically and mentally.

Do not be discouraged if at first you experience no response or elation—if the exercise is carried out with care ten or fifteen minutes daily, at the end of a week you will be astonished at your progress.

The colours of nature have a cosmic vitality which

artificial colours do not possess, but failing access to the colour-screen of nature you can employ substitute means of developing your colour-faculty. The Chinese, who are a race naturally sensitive to colour, not uncommonly introduce into their homes in the squalid districts of London and San Francisco, the glorious ethereal colours of their own radiant land. They turn a room into a sanctuary of colour, by the use of screens, draperies, china ornaments, gay lanterns, flowers, wall-paper or distemper.

Surely we could emulate our oriental brothers !

Not only should we be conscious of the colour vibrations in our environment but we should also remember that every individual is a living, mobile colour-screen. In other words, we are perpetually projecting, by means of our auras, rays and emanations of colour from our inner selves. Our auras shine with vitality and brightness or are obscured with grey thought-clouds according to our degree of evolution. Bear this in mind when you are dealing or mixing with people—consider whether you are radiating a bright, cheerful personality, or a dull drab one.

If you project colour only in a minor degree you enjoy only a limited vitality and you cannot do justice to yourself. If your aura is obscured you will be either unhappy, frustrated or leading a negative, mechanical existence.

You will naturally ask—" can anything be done to improve a negative aura, and to project more colour into one's personality."

The Cosmic teachings show us that a great deal can be achieved in this direction once we understand the nature of the cosmic forces that surround us and their relation to our personality and environment.

If you make a strong effort to project your own colour vibrations with the utmost intensity you can amalgamate them with the Cosmic currents, participating in their life and thereby augmenting your own vitality.

The vast ocean of consciousness in which we live is vibrating with life and is capable of receiving and transmitting thought. In the Cosmic Soul and Mind there are currents of thought and streams of psychic energy similar to the currents in the ocean—we can and do attach ourselves either consciously or unconsciously to different currents. You can draw from the Cosmic Mind such thought and ideas as you are in harmony with.

The Cosmic Rays or currents are spiritual forces emanating from the Divine White Light. From the occult point of view, we are surrounded by etheric forces and radiations which are essential for our existence, just as our physical bodies are surrounded by air, vital to life.

It is an axiom of occultism, that Force is One, but force or energy manifests on this planet under seven major aspects—these are the seven cosmic rays, or vibrating currents. Although basically there is only one Ultimate Ray, we are conscious of seven aspects of it, due to the different rates of vibrations. Each of these seven Rays is subdivided into other rays or currents of force.

The Cosmic Rays cannot be adequately or correctly described by our earth-language but for practical purposes we designate them as vibrations appearing, *as near as possible, as* Red, Orange, Yellow, Green, Blue, Indigo and Violet. It is important to remember that Cosmic Colour was the first substantial force in the Universe—it preceded all other forms of matter, life and substance, just as light precedes the manifestation of a new day. Space was a void of negative darkness before the Cosmic Light appeared.

The Cosmic Rays are coeval and coexistent with the history of the world. Some mystics and developed sensitives of a high order have perceived the primordial light and colour and it has been dimly seen by men under the name of " zodiacal light."

The Cosmic currents are perpetually vibrating not only

on the surface of the earth but also, above and through it, encircling the globe in streams of endless, inexhaustible energy. As in the macrocosm so also in the microcosm— the same rays and forces surround and permeate every human being. The human mind can attach itself to the Cosmic Rays—the Red, Blue, Green, Yellow current as the case may be—and attract and receive its powers and blessings.

The first thing to do to become conscious of the Cosmic Colour currents is to visualise them mentally—and by concentrating you will open the door of knowledge and will thereby consciously understand. You will first become sensitive to the Solar vibrations—the ordinary rays of the spectrum—and you will later feel conscious of the Universal Rays as your Colour-faculty develops.

> " When the Wisdom-light (the Aura) streameth
> forth from all the Gates of the Body (the chakras)
> then it may be known that Harmony (Cosmic
> Consciousness) is increasing."

CHAPTER VII

THE TEMPLE OF COLOUR

ONE of the most lovely and inspiring experiences to which every diligent student of the Radiant Science may attain is contact with the Temple of Colour. This is not a human or material building, but a degree of consciousness in which the mind is raised to the higher Astral.

The Astral Sphere, with its sub-planes, is accessible to seekers who have reached a certain stage in their wisdom-studies. Like all the other planes which surround us, it contains good and bad, high and low, inferior and superior states of being, but those who penetrate to it are at once attracted to their counterparts, and enter appropriate regions according to the condition of their Auras. It is a realm of great Beauty, Light and Colour.

On the upper regions of the Astral plane the great Masters, Teachers and Guides of humanity from still higher spheres have established a centre or meeting-place where human souls can be met, and taught the higher Truths. It is chiefly from this high astral centre that dwellers on the Earth acquire advanced wisdom, inspiration and healing power. In the ancient writings it is spoken of as the Temple of Knowledge. Here are stored and preserved the true records of every race, country and tribe that ever existed, every vestige of which has long since perished from the earth. All the knowledge that man has gained, or ever will gain, is to be found in this Temple—all ideas, truths, wisdom and science are enshrined within the vastness of this astral University.

An essential part of this wonderful centre of Light is the Temple of Colour. There is no true counterpart of this in the physical world. The eyes of the ordinary beholder, unaccustomed to the study of cosmic colour-vibrations, would be blinded by the unparalleled splendour and intensity of the radiations. Very probably they might say that they could see nothing, because everything to them would appear hidden by a cloud of mist.

A more perfect environment for the Temple of Colour cannot be imagined. The feeling which the earth-dweller gets in reaching this indescribably peaceful and secluded region is one of the highest exhilaration. The glorious temple rises gracefully from the soft green sward on which it stands. The ethereal beauty of the spot and the sublime colouring can scarcely be judged by our terrestrial standards.

The Temple itself is entirely screened by a crescent of tall, beautiful trees, whose green radiations at once inspire a feeling of harmony and tranquillity. In front of the magnificent building lies an oval lake which reflects like a gigantic mirror the whole scene of exquisite splendour.

The Temple is cruciform in shape, and is crowned by a large golden dome, with a slender tapering spire of glistening white, which symbolises the Great White Light of the Eternal Logos. The four main divisions of the Temple are curved and rounded in shape, and shine with a brilliant radiance, the curves of the roof arches and windows flow and join together in perfect proportion.

The entire edifice shines and glows with living Colour—one unconsciously absorbs the vital health-giving vibrations. Unlike earth buildings, there is no impression of materiality whatever in the construction—it is as though the Divine Architect had assembled together the opalescent mists and colouring of a summer sunset.

From the front view of the building one sees seven graceful minarets tapering upwards, each representing one of the Seven Great Rays. The tall luminous columns glow with life and colour. The glorious sparkling crimson Ray sends out continuous emanations of life and love, the flaming, scintillating Orange Ray pours out the tonic-force of health and uplifting vitality. The third column is radiant with flashing, golden streams of awakening light—the Yellow Ray of mind, whilst the central column, as though conscious of its position as the Ray of Balance, emits refreshing, calm, emanations of peace and harmony—the Green Ray. Next is the inspiring Blue column, flashing with tints of heavenly azure and sapphire, the shining Ray of Truth and inspiration. The last two columns of colour appear as towers of mystery and enchantment, so completely transcendent and indescribable are their variegated tints of Indigo, Purple and Violet.

This Astral spectrum is brighter than any collection of colours to be seen on the earth plane. The seven radiant columns blend and combine to form an exquisite display of colour, of far greater beauty than our Rainbow.

Within the glorious building the same sublime beauty is manifested. Words cannot describe the glories of the Temple of Colour, but a description of one of the services conducted therein may prove interesting and instructive.

Each of the four portions into which the Temple is divided is devoted to a service of a particular kind. The principle of the astral Temple is to act on each individual according to his especial "type," or the stage of his development. It is realised that every person has some special channel linking him with the Divine. In some it manifests as love, service, and brotherhood, in others, devotion and inspiration, in others, sympathy and healing, whilst in some it appears as intellectual power.

There are four types of services or developing ceremonies corresponding to the above groups. The Teacher acts as a medium or intermediary between the candidate and the Logos, receiving, concentrating and transmitting the streams of spiritual force, and distributing and applying the sublime vibrations of light and colour.

In the service of the Red Ray, the candidate first closes his eyes, and with the outer senses stilled and passive, visualises mentally a flood or cloud of colour. The Teacher stands within the pyramid of concentration, in front of the candidates. He materialises in a glorious human form, clothed in a resplendent crimson vestment. The beholder perceives an awe-inspiring flashing of brilliant colours, like rays above his head. Words fail to describe properly this band or spectrum of colour. It is different from any physical or material spectrum, presenting a dazzling appearance like the midday sun, and is vitalised with the astral light. It is more than a focus of light, as it is really a thought-form expressed in the astral colour-language. Actually, it is a manifestation of the vibrational key-note of the particular service, indicating the nature and object of the point to be attained.

Each candidate strives to imitate the vibrational key-note by projecting above his own head a similar but smaller spectrum of colour. The lights emanating from each student vary greatly—some are able to produce an excellent replica of that manifested by the Teacher, whilst some produce only feeble glimmerings. The aim is to make it visible on the physical plane—the majority of candidates are only able to manifest the power on the astral and mental planes.

The teacher extends his arms over the assembly, and sends out a stream of power, over all present. The spiritual outflow enters their auras in exact correspondence with their own colour-forms and stage of development— it influences and uplifts them in the same ratio.

This outpouring of power is not merely the personal emanation of the Teacher—the real source is from the Temple of Higher Teachers and Instructors—the Teacher is only the channel for these wondrous forces. It is difficult to describe adequately the astral effect of this service. The Aura of the officiating Teacher becomes a vast sea of pale crimson light, which spreads out in ever-widening waves over the whole assembly. Each candidate projects his own personal colour-ray into the rose-coloured aura, presenting a striking effect of subsidiary flames and tongues of colour, piercing the deeper and wide-spreading crimson sea.

It is a picture of marvellous glory. The vast aura eventually includes the entire assembly within it—the power is absorbed by each individual.

After a certain time has elapsed and the Teacher judges that all the conditions are tuned to the same vibration, he revises the flow of force, and concentrates his Aura into a smaller spherical form with a great column reaching upwards. He then raises his arms above his head, and each candidate sends towards the Teacher his concentrated affection and aspiration. The Teacher absorbs all these rays of love and spiritual desire, and pours them upwards in a column of gorgeous colours, like an opalescent fountain. It flows through the Higher Beings in the upper Spiritual planes until it reaches the Great One, the Supreme Logos.

The response from on high comes speedily back. For a moment the Light of the Logos shines forth—a stupendous, unutterable brilliancy. It flashes like a blaze of meteoric splendour in a winter's night, down through the planes until it touches the Teacher expectant on the dais. He lowers his arms and extends them over the assembly. The hushed temple is filled with a flood of divine splendour—a sea of gorgeous colours suffuses the silent concourse, then into each individual aura flows the power and the glory, the message of Divine love and blessing. The immediate effect of this down-flow of Divine power is to make every candidate realise for the moment the essential divinity within himself, his inborn divine capacities, his link with the life of God.

The candidate himself becomes charged for the time with divine power, enabling him to help and uplift his fellowmen. All sensitive people are conscious of the radiations sent forth from the Astral Temple. Each service releases beneficent, healing thought-forms, which are absorbed by numerous people and are made use of by spiritual healers everywhere. Just as the release of atomic energy causes vast and widespread devastation and bombards whole districts with deadly radiations for a considerable time, so the release of Divine energy suffuses the world, and keeps up a steady radiation of Love and Healing upon all who are in harmony with the Eternal Good.

PART II

GUIDE TO COLOUR-HEALING

CHAPTER I

THE COSMIC HEALING RAYS

NATURE has provided seven main Colour Rays for the treatment of disease. The Colour Rays are representatives of the pure cosmic radiance : they are in essence spiritual forces perpetually flowing round and through the earth.

As explained in the following chapter, colour vibrations work through the chakras or cosmic centres of the body. The principle behind Colour-Healing is the regulation of the flow of the colour forces by consciously absorbing them as needed, using each ray with the specific purpose of rebuilding, restoring, and re-vitalising every organ of the body through the etheric counterparts.

Regular and systematic practice will gradually transform your body, mind and spirit. The general health will improve, the mind will become more efficient and the spirit-self more sensitive and developed. The Cosmic Colour System soon becomes a subconscious functioning— Colour being one of the fundamental elements in the universe acts directly on the subconscious mind which strongly affects the health, vitality and harmony of life.

RAY 1 IS THE RED COSMIC RAY.

This Ray is found at the thermal or heat end of the spectrum : thus, by its very nature it is stimulating and warming. The power of Red to stimulate the arterial blood is shown not only in drugs which belong to the red group but also in cases of healing by red light. In the human body this colour controls the chakram at the base of the spine and exercises great influence upon the health and vitality of the body. Red rays cause reaction to occur in this centre resulting in the release of adrenalin into the bloodstream. Red light increases the amount of haemo-globin in the blood and improves the circulation by raising the temperature of the body. Red is thus the natural antidote to the cold blue conditions which it counteracts. Foods that help the Red Ray are beet, radishes, red cabbage, cresses, spinach, plums and damsons, black cherries, berries and currants.

The effect of Red on the mental and nervous system is stimulating and uplifting. Red, being the colour of the life-force, engenders strength, courage, and enthusiasm. The best shade to cultivate mentally and physically is Rose-red, the symbol of Universal Love.

The Red Ray may be applied in all cases of blood disorders, weak or impaired vitality, debility and depletion and defective circulation: also for depression, fear and worry.

RAY 2 IS THE ORANGE COSMIC RAY.

This Ray is of very great value as it is linked with the vital force that flows into the body from the sun. It con-trols the chakram in the spleen and is concerned with the task of absorbing and distributing the vital energy.

Orange Rays influence the processes of digestion and assimilation. The colour is a powerful tonic and has a direct effect in building the energy of the body.

Being the middle ray between the physical and mental principles, Orange is of vital importance mentally in the assimilation and visualisation of ideas. This Ray is an excellent antidote to repressions and limitations and calls forth self-confidence and positive thinking: hence its value in salesmanship and display.

It is a plus-vibration and care must be exercised in its use as it can lead to over-stimulation. It is always advisable to blend or modify a very strong vibration with one of lesser potency that is in harmony with it—in this case Blue and Yellow or Green.

The effect of Orange on the mind is to foster optimism, courage and the will to succeed. The Orange Ray is used in the treatment of the spleen and kidneys : also bronchitis, chest conditions and venous debility.

RAY 3 IS THE YELLOW COSMIC RAY.

Yellow holds the first place in the spectrum for maximum brightness and luminosity. It is the Ray of maximum light and is a positive magnetic vibration with a powerful effect on the nervous system. It is connected with the Solar Plexus the chakram which acts as the brain centre of the nervous system. This Ray has affinity with the liver and intestines and has a cleansing and healing effect on the skin.

It is one of the " Rays of Mind " and certainly stimulates the mental faculties, helping in the creation of thought and in visualisation.

As a general colour it arouses optimism, cheerfulness and a balanced outlook on life. It is an excellent colour to have in a room where mental pursuits are carried out.

This Ray is used in the treatment of the organs that are adjacent to the Solar Plexus as well as diseases of the skin and nerves.

RAY 4 IS THE GREEN COSMIC RAY.

The Green Ray occupies the middle or point of balance in the solar spectrum. It is midway between the thermal or heat end of the spectrum and the cold or electric end. Hence, it is the Ray of Balance, Harmony and Concord.

Green is the colour of Nature and is a soothing harmonious radiation that is essential for the well-being of our nerves and the proper functioning of the body. The " Green Pasture " and fresh air philosophy is not a poetical fancy but a stark necessity.

This Ray controls the chakram at the heart or cardiac centre. Green light being composed of Yellow and Blue rays strongly influences the blood-pressure and heart action : the blue element in it counterbalances the more potent energy of the Yellow Ray. Green light gives us the energy of the sun in the safest and most natural form and is identical with the green plant-energy known as chlorophyll which is prescribed by medical science as a specific for the heart. This Ray radiates sympathy, kindness, peace and is also linked with abundance, evolution and supply. Green in any form is one of the finest tonics for tired nerves. The shade or " chroma " should be bright and clear, but much will depend on individual preferences.

This Ray is used in the treatment of diseases of the heart and blood and is also useful for the nerves of the head.

RAY 5 IS THE BLUE RAY.

Blue is the first colour belonging to the cold, non-stimulating or astringent division of the spectrum. Its effect is to steady or slow-down the energy of the Red-Orange-Yellow group. It successfully combats feverish conditions, bleeding, germs, nervous irritation, etc.

Psychologically, the Blue vibration raises the consciousness to the realm of spirit : hence the value of this colour in spiritual healing, meditation, devotional services and so on. The Cosmic Soul or higher mind of nature expresses much of the peace, beauty and harmony of creation through the Blue and Green Rays. This Ray has a calming effect on the mind and nerves and is successfully employed in cases of insomnia.

Truth, peace, poise and serenity are the main features of the mental influence of the Blue Ray.

It is connected with the chakram at the throat and is

used in the treatment of diseased conditions of that region :
also in fevers, rheumatism and headaches.

RAY 6 IS THE INDIGO COSMIC RAY.

The Indigo Ray is of high value as an astringent, purifying and cooling vibration. It is based on a very important
glandular centre—the Pineal—which is concerned with the
nervous, mental and psychic forces and faculties of man.
The organs of sight, hearing and smelling are under the
influence of the Indigo Ray.

This Ray provides one of the safest and most natural
anaesthetics causing an hypnotic condition in which the
patient is insensitive to pain yet at the same time fully
conscious.

Stimulating and regenerating to the mind and soul,
Indigo is one of the rays of the future race-consciousness
extending the inner vision and opening up new fields of
comprehension and knowledge. Acting on the personality
and character it is an antidote to frustrations, the fear-
complex and general negative conditions.

Among the numerous diseases that are successfully
treated with Indigo are mental disorders, especially obses-
sions, nervous disorders, insomnia, and diseases of the eye,
ear and nose.

RAY 7 IS THE VIOLET COSMIC RAY.

Violet is the highest vibration of Light, with strong
electro-chemical properties, and the rays are stimulating
to the nervous system. It is inspiring to the mind, arousing
soul-qualities, mysticism, spiritual intuition and idealism.
It is useful for restoring the mental equilibrium and lack
of poise which the rush and bustle of modern life produces
in so many sensitive people. It is not a colour for the
masses but appeals more to the sensitive and soul-con-
scious type of person. Its two divisions, the Purple and the

Amethyst, correspond to the material and spiritual aspects.

The absorption of Purple or Violet light for a short time each evening will be found invaluable for brain-workers and will help considerably in ensuring restful sleep.

The Violet Ray is connected with the chakram in the higher brain known as the Pituitary Gland which is concerned with the spiritual intuitive faculty. This colour aids the development of the spiritual consciousness, clairvoyance and psychic sensitiveness and is of great value in meditation and concentration exercises.

Violet is used in the treatment of mental, nervous and cerebral diseases, neurosis, neuralgia, rheumatism and epilepsy.

CHAPTER II

THE COLOUR CHAKRAS

THE term *chakra* is of Hindu origin and means literally
" wheel of fire." The term is used to designate the dynamic centres of vital force and consciousness—the gener-
ators of prana and the inlets of cosmic energy into the
human system.

There are seven main chakras each under a particular
colour-ray. The chakras form a system of *colour* in the
physical and etheric bodies as follows :—

> Chakra 1. Red. Situated at the base of the spine.
> Chakra 2. Orange. In the region of the spleen.
> Chakra 3. Yellow. Solar Plexus.
> Chakra 4. Green. Region of the heart.
> Chakra 5. Blue. The throat centre. (Thyroid gland).
> Chakra 6. Indigo. Pineal gland.
> Chakra 7. Violet. Pituitary body.

The chakras are seen clairvoyantly as radiant bell-
shaped vortices in the etheric body—the vital counterpart
of the physical. These vortices intersect the spinal cord at
certain definite points.

We have seen that solar energy is the source of all forms
of energy in our universe. Scientists have discerned that
in sunlight there exist certain particles which contain a
special vital and stimulatory force. These particles are
termed *vitality globules*. Eastern occultists have long
known these globules of life under the generic name of
prana which literally means breath, or life.

In the human body prana is specialised by each individual when it is drawn into the body from the atmosphere

through the chakras and distributed over the whole system. The vital energy in prana is present in every cell and molecule of the body.

It should be noted that the Red and Orange Chakras which govern the physical and etheric aspects in man are very closely related and are sometimes classed together as a single unit. The size and configuration of the chakras depend on the type of individual and the general stage of development. The more highly evolved the astral, mental and spiritual aspects are the clearer and more definite the chakras become and the more perfect their colours. Concisely speaking, they are the etheric organs working through thought and feeling directly upon the physical body.

The chakras are specialised channels of colour-force. Each chakra absorbs a special current of vital energy through its particular Colour Ray from the physical environment and from higher levels of consciousness. The Orange Chakra for instance draws in the *prana* of the physical atmosphere, i.e. the sunlight with its life-giving vitality globules. The vital energy of the Orange Ray is then absorbed and distributed to all parts of the body.

Whilst the higher prana-energy is not inhaled through the lungs the activity of the Orange Chakra is directly associated with breathing—its activity is determined by the breathing rhythm which increases the absorption of vitality globules.

Deep rhythmic breathing is of great value. It enables us to draw in a much greater supply of physical prana than the shallow uncontrolled form of breathing. The most beneficial form is Colour Breathing. It will be found most vitalising and uplifting and a general tonic for tired minds and nerves.

In Colour Breathing one mentally visualises the life-giving radiations of Colour pouring in from the atmosphere surrounding us. The simplest way is to sit in a chair before an open window (whenever possible). Slowly relax the body by bending forward, holding the arms limp, and exhale all the air from the lungs. Then breathe in slowly, as you assume an upright position, focusing your mind on the Indigo Chakra (the pineal gland within the forehead). Hold the breath whilst you count from one to twelve calmly and unhurriedly.

You will soon find that the counting becomes automatic whilst your conscious mind dwells on the thought of new power, life and harmony flooding your entire being. Later on, as you make progress it is greatly beneficial to breathe deeply and in rhythm to a universal statement, visualising as clearly as you can the colour you desire to make manifest in your aura.

The great advantage of this simple exercise is that it replenishes your whole being through the chakras with new life and also develops the power of cosmic colour perception.

Occult Science teaches that the supply of prana is greater in direct light : it is nonetheless true however that deep rhythmic breathing in coloured light also increases the flow of vitality.

Thirty seconds of deep breathing can effect a change in the appearance of the health-aura transforming it from grey or leaden-colour to deep blue, strengthening the emanations and restoring them from a bent and drooping condition to shining rays of power and health.

The chakras influence the appropriate centres on different planes. Each one acts as a channel for a particular influence from one or other of the psychological centres. Thus the Orange Chakra at the splenic centre influences the emotional or astral nature of man as also does the Yellow Chakra in a greater or lesser degree. It should be remembered that no two individuals are exactly alike.

The psychological influences vary exceedingly and the activity of the chakras is not strictly localised but is inter-penetrative.

Strictly speaking, the Yellow Chakra (solar Plexus) is the centre of the lower mind (objective, material) and is also complicated by emotional influences. Golden yellow is the colour of intellect in its higher phases and aspects. The Green Chakra (heart) registers impulses of the higher mind (subjective, abstract aspect) and also higher emotions such as compassion and sympathy.

The Blue Chakra (throat) is the gateway of the spiritual aspect in man. It is centre of the religious instinct, the devotional and mystical nature. When working in harmony with the Red and Yellow Chakras there is peace and balance in body and mind. It is the region of the causal body—the root-cause of your present condition of life.

The two higher chakras are super-rational and trans-cendental : their full activity is found only in initiates and highly-developed souls.

The Indigo Chakra presides over the higher phenomena of the soul—sensitivity, colour perception and spiritual intuition, true clairvoyance, healing, etc. Its root-centre is in the pineal gland. Allied to it and really an extension of it is the Violet Chakra at the crown of the head—the sanctuary of the spirit and the gateway of the highest influences in man. Its material counterpart is the pituitary body.

CHAPTER III

METHODS OF COLOUR TREATMENT

COLOUR-THERAPY. LAMP RADIATION.

ONE of the best ways of using Colour for the treatment of specified ills or for the restoration of health is by employing some simple apparatus, such as an electric Colour Lamp or some coloured glass. The latter is somewhat difficult to obtain now but simple colour lamps are procurable. They are made to focus the seven rays as required.

Whatever type of light-projector is used the same principles apply. There are two main kinds of Ray treatment, viz.:—General diffusion, and Local concentration. In general diffusion the light-rays are focused on the body, especially the back, the region of the spine and nervous system. General diffusion is excellent for re-charging the tired nerve-cells with new life. The patient either sits or lies down in a relaxed position, stripped to the waist, and is wholly immersed in the light for thirty minutes. Colour treatment by lamps should not exceed this period. An auxilary to general diffusion is Radiant Magnetism.

In local concentration the light is focused on the affected area only. The great value of colour-therapy lies in the penetrative power of light. Light and Colour have a direct action on the protoplasm of the body—the speed and power of the chemical reactions depend upon the biological state of the organism.

Radiation is still a subject that is little understood and the penetrating properties of certain cosmic rays are even more marvellous than those of light. The Cosmic Rays rain upon the earth in continuous showers from outer space and contain charged-particles of enormous energy. Their

74

penetrating power is so great that the rays have been detected in mines 3,000 feet under the earth.

Exactly how light penetrates or influences the body is not easy to comprehend. One view is that a permeation of the cells takes place as in ordinary osmosis. The most favoured view however is that light and colour influence the body by arousing sympathetic vibrations within the organism. In other words light and colour work according to the Law of Attraction.

In studying the nature of light it is important to remember that all radiations emitted from a luminous body travel through space in perfect rhythmic vibrations in the form of waves. The point or distance from crest to crest is called the wave-length and their " best " or rate of vibration is known as their frequency. Colours have varying wave-lengths. For instance violet consists of very short waves, while Red has much longer ones. These facts are important in treating disease. The deep, slow, warming vibration of Red-light stimulates and invigorates the system while the shorter and higher Violet and Blue waves calm and pacify.

As a wave of light is projected through space it creates a certain rhythm—an harmonious vibration of etheric matter. When light and colour strike a surface the homogeneous particles are thrown into sympathetic vibration with the incoming current : as a result the organism is vitalised and re-charged. If however the particles within the body are non-conductive or of an opposite rate of vibration, or if the power of the incoming current is too strong, then an abnormal reaction will occur which may produce serious harm or damage. It is very important for the healer to know the nature of the light or colour he uses—its quality, quantity or intensity.

The essence of Colour-healing consists in causing certain molecular reactions in the organism or vital centres through the medium of the rays. Light, it should be remembered, is not a force or energy outside us—light enters into the centre of every cell, nerve and tissue of our bodies. Nature has given us this wonderful form of energy which is the basis of life, to maintain our minds and bodies alike in perfect health.

COLOUR BREATHING.

Just as the invisible radiations of the sun and the Cosmic Rays surround us on all sides, so also the very air we breathe is permeated with the forces of light and colour. This vital energy, or *prana*, as the Hindus call it, is the living force that imparts and sustains life. We extract it from the food we eat, from the water we drink and most of all from the air we breathe. When we absorb large quantities of prana we enjoy good health and vitality.

What we call " fresh air " consists of much more than just oxygen and other chemical ingredients. It contains radiations from the sun, from the far-off stars and planets as well as from the earth. Air is the outer vehicle of prana and other forces. The Colour Healer therefore practises deep rhythmic breathing with visualisation of the rays absorbing them into his body and inner principles. He also teaches his patients to practise deep breathing, and to make simple mental affirmations expressive of the Ray being drawn upon.

The Colour Healer is always a deep breather. He is always conscious of the Universal Life-Spirit that is about him to strengthen him and with each deep inbreathing he draws into himself a portion of this power. He does this consciously feeling the grandeur of being in harmony with the Infinite. When he eats it is with the feeling that he is taking sustenance into his body which is adding to his reserve force. When he sleeps it is with the knowledge that he entrusts himself to the beneficent action of Divine

Energy in rebuilding the exhausted cells of the body and inspiring him for the tasks of the next day.

The following exercise will be found most useful and beneficial. Sit comfortably in a chair before an open window : close your eyes and when you have contemplated in the mind for three minutes on the desired colour, bend forward and expel all the air from your lungs and stomach, making the body as limp as possible. All the muscles must be relaxed so that each limb is perfectly limp and as far as possible forgotten. Then take one deep inbreathing beginning with the expansion of the abdomen and carrying the breath up by one continued inspiration inhalation to the ribs and chest. As you breathe in count up to eight : then hold the breath for another eight seconds and lastly exhale during eight more seconds.

The best time to practise is immediately following or preceding breakfast and supper. The exercise should not be practised last thing at night during the first month as it is definitely stimulating and the increase of vital force may take some time to get accustomed to. It is important to feel conscious during this exercise of the inflow of the rays re-vitalising the whole system and replenishing the finer vehicles with cosmic energy. Controlled breathing not only raises the bodily vibrations but unites us subjectively with the Universal Consciousness.

Each of the seven rays may be breathed in according to the specific need. It is well to remember that the first three Colour Rays, i.e., Red, Orange, Yellow, are magnetic, and should be visualised as flowing up from the earth towards the solar plexus. The last three—Blue, Indigo, Violet—are electrical and are breathed in from the ether downwards. The Green Ray—the balancer of the spectrum—flows into the system horizontally.

RADIANT MAGNETISM.

Many scientists who have studied the invisible forces

of the human system have come to the conclusion that the body is similar to a magnet. Reichenbach, Dr. Kilner, Dr. Baraduc, Dr. Babbitt and others speak of the luminous emanations which have been seen flowing from the fingertips of healers and sensitives. The hands are the main source of healing magnetism and are the channels of the seven rays.

To quote the words of Dr. Gregory, author of *Animal Magnetism* : " The human body is found to possess the same influence and to produce the same effects as magnets. I have already spoken of the light seen to issue from the tips of the operator's fingers. The hands are oppositely polar, and the head, eyes and mouth are also foci where the auric influence seems to be concentrated." (Page 100, *Animal Magnetism*.)

The right, or positive hand, is used for transmitting the healing vibrations into the patient's body : the left or negative hand is used to close the circuit and also to draw off the negative conditions of the patient. The value of the hand in healing is well expressed by Dr. Coates in his book, *Human Magnetism* : " The human hand is used instinctively in the alleviation of pain and in the cure of disease. The whole process is perfectly natural whether applied to self-healing or to the healing of others. If a person suffers from cramp in the stomach, in the side or in a limb, immediately the hand flies to the spot, and by rubbing, manipulation of and about the region affected, the cramp is removed. In headache and in toothache the involuntary application of the hand is a common occurrence. The operation is hereditary or instinctive so that in spite of scepticism I have known a doctor nurse his own head or jaw, seeking relief in this manner, and while it is probable that he was not in a condition to benefit himself, yet another person in a state of health and possessed of sufficient sympathy, laying hands on the affected part could give help and perhaps cure the disease."

Dr. Coates was able to put restless and sleepless patients to sleep by merely laying his hand upon their brows. " The hand soothed pain and the hand gave sleep : therefore from the hand or by the hand was conveyed to the sufferer something which was needed, something also that I was fortunately able to impart." (Page 114, *Human Magnetism.*)

The advanced healer can consciously direct the correct colour-current through his sensitive hands. As a general rule the right hand should be placed over the solar plexus, whilst the left hand is held over the chakram or glandular centre requiring healing treatment.

The solar plexus is a great nerve-centre exercising an important influence on the health. The application of the positive hand on this plexus causes the healing ray to radiate through the entire nervo-vital system from head to foot—thence it sets in the direction of the healer's left hand seeking to complete the circuit. When the healer feels that the circuit has been completed he withdraws his left hand from the spinal centre or wherever it may be resting and allows the colour-vibration to flow into his patient from the right hand alone. This may take from one to five minutes. After a short pause he taps the centre or organ with the tip of the third finger of his left hand. This causes a flow of colour-magnetism to the point of contact and should result in a sensation similar to a mild current of electricity. The healer allows his finger to rest in one place for a few seconds and then proceeds to touch the spinal cord from end to end. This should continue for five minutes.

It is important to administer the treatment with warm hands—if cold they should be first rubbed briskly together before applying them to the patient. In all treatments the patient should close his eyes and cultivate a relaxed condition of mind and body.

THE COLOUR PASS.

For receiving this treatment the patient sits comfortably in a chair, thoroughly relaxed, with eyes closed. A few words on relaxation may be given before the commencement. The healer then stands in front of the patient and concentrates on the colour he wishes to transmit. He makes a mental affirmation such as : " I will restore colour and health to this patient," or, " I will relieve the patient of his pain. I will transmit such-or-such colour ray to restore his nervous system to harmony."

While so concentrating, he slowly raises both hands, with the fingers clenched, and in a wide sweep raises them above the patient's head, bringing them together and unclenching the fingers at a point just above his forehead. He next spreads his fingers out a little and very slowly brings them down past the forehead, face, chest, abdomen, to the knees, taking a full thirty seconds for the movement. The healer's body follows the downward sweep of the hands. After the complete pass shake the hands to throw off the negative vibrations of the patient, then clench the fingers again and repeat the process. The treatment should be continued for five minutes.

This is an ideal way to transmit colour-vibrations when apparatus is lacking. Remember that the Red and Orange Rays increase the vitality, the Yellow Rays supply nerve-power, the Green Rays soothe and energise, the Blue Rays induce calmness and spiritual inspiration bringing the higher consciousness into activity.

The hands are the only instruments used in this general treatment for transferring colour to a patient and both hands should be employed in every case.

COLOUR-CHARGED CLOTHS.

When treating patients living at a distance it is a great aid in supplementing the absent treatment to forward a piece of cloth polarised to the individual healing ray. Take a piece of coloured silk or cloth about the size of a post-card and sprinkle it with a few drops of water on both sides. Place it between the palms of your hands for two minutes concentrating your mind upon it and willing strongly that the colour rays shall be absorbed and passed on to our patient. It should be sent wrapped in clean paper and should be worn by the patient on the part of the body requiring treatment. No one but the patient should handle the magnetised cloth.

Regarding the magnetisation of objects, Dr. Babbitt states : " In cool weather when the air is electrical I can make one, two or three strokes over tissue or other paper, and throwing it into the air within a foot of the wall, it will spring to it like a thing of life and cling there for hours, sometimes even for days. A mere stroke will make it attractive of everything around it, although it will generally repel another magnetised sheet, unless this sheet is mag-netised with the same stroke as they lie together. Thous-ands of others can do the same thing and some better than myself." (*Principles of Light and Colour*, page 429.)

MAGNETISED WATER.

Most patients derive benefit from water that has been magnetised or ray-charged. Take a glass and fill it with cold water : hold the glass in the left hand and place the right hand over it with the fingers and thumb pointing downwards over the surface of the water but not touching it. Now concentrate upon the healing colour you desire to instil into the water. Five minutes' concentration will magnetise a glass of water with colour-vibrations. The patient should take the water in doses of a wine-glassful every half hour for the first day, every hour for the second day, and a wine-glassful three times a day to finish the treatment.

As an interesting experiment it is suggested that the

healer sets two glasses of water before a patient, one of which has been magnetised, and allow him to distinguish between the two. Patients usually declare that the magnetised water has a slightly metallic taste.

WARM INSUFFLATION. (A very ancient healing method.)

The vital force contained in the breath has previously been mentioned. The mouth being a focus of human magnetism and colour radiation, the advanced healer is able to transmit healing force by breathing upon the patient. Warm insufflation is given by breathing upon a piece of flannel laid upon the affected area. The healer places his mouth close against the flannel and by breathing heavily upon it causes heat-vibrations to be felt in the part. The breathing is continued several minutes. This method is found effective in relieving many forms of nerve pains, such as headaches, neuralgia and rheumatism—in fact, any acute pain. Chronic constipation also responds to the breathing treatment. Place a piece of flannel about six inches square on the bare skin over the solar plexus. Bend over the patient and apply your left hand to the lumbar (lower) region of the spine so that the patient lies upon that hand.

Now breathe through the flannel with the mouth upon it, inhaling air through the nostrils. The magnetic radiation has an immediate effect on the peristaltic action and will overcome a habit of constipation of many years' standing.

SOLARISED FOODS.

One of the best ways of absorbing colour is the judicious use of vegetables, fruit and liquids that have been suncharged. Fruit and vegetables are the direct result of the sun's radiation. The Colour Healer, therefore studies the different groups of vegetables and fruit and classifies them according to the Rays to which they belong.

People need a constant replenishment of the particular rate of energy indicated by their Ray. Thus people who are polarised to the Orange Ray and who are thereby specially prone to suffer from nervous debility, kidney and splenic troubles, require plenty of Orange Ray vegetables and fruit, such as carrots, swedes, oranges, peaches. The juices and liquid extracts from these food-groups are also highly valuable.

The guiding principle in diet should be to eat the finer kinds of foods as much as possible in preference to coarse foods and to seek first those foods that contain most of the Cosmic Solar Energy.

HEALING BOWLS AND JARS.

To those who do not scorn to learn from the past, I would like to mention a healing device practised by the Ancient Egyptians. The mysterious people of the Nile who worshipped the Sun as a symbol of Deity knew also the power of the solar rays to rebuild the health. The priests used bowls in which the juices of certain fruits and vegetables were first expressed, and then set them out in the sun to become charged with the " energy of Ra."

They sometimes encrusted the healing bowls with jewels of the same colour as the fruit or vegetable being used to add a still greater potency. Nowadays the Colour Healer follows the same principle by using coloured glass jars corresponding to the fruit or the Rays required for the cure.

CHAPTER IV

MENTAL AND ABSENT HEALING

IN the Cosmic System of Healing the use of Colour is combined with the force of Mind. The mental factor in health and disease is fully recognised. The true Colour Healer sees different levels of consciousness, such as the etheric, the mental, the causal and the spiritual, all of which contribute in their final working out to the state of either harmony or disease in the physical.

The Colour Healer is aware that the infinite powers of Spirit manifesting in the White Light flows into each individual through the magnetic aura. In the degree to which the aura reciprocates to the divine inflow so personal harmony and well-being is the result. In the case of spiritual, emotional or etheric maladjustments appearing in the personality in various forms such as emotional and nervous tension, feelings of bitterness, resentment, frustration, hatred and the mental complexes of fear, worry, inferiority, selfishness, etc., the divine inflow of Love, Health and Harmony does not reach the centre of man's being. It is stopped through wrong thinking or the wrong vibration or wrong action with the result that a blank area, so to speak, is formed, which swiftly becomes the breeding-ground of negative, evil or undivine thoughts and elements which work themselves out as diseased conditions of all kinds.

Just as the root or plant that cannot catch the sunlight becomes a stunted, faded, undeveloped organism, so the individual who is cut off from the White Light of Spirit becomes ill and defective, a victim of his own false or perverted mind.

The main characteristic of true mind or intelligence is

responsiveness, recognition, and the whole action of the Universal or Cosmic Mind in bringing the evolutionary process from its first beginnings to its present human stage is achieved by a continual intelligent response which the demand which each stage in the progress has made for an adjustment between itself and its environment.

The Colour healer recognises a universal intelligence permeating all things and also sees a corresponding responsiveness hidden deep down in their nature and ready to be called into action when appealed to.

Colour Treatment is based on the principle that all healing is a change of mental attitude or belief.

The subconscious or subjective mind is the creative faculty within us and creates whatever the conscious mind impresses upon it. The conscious mind, the vehicle of the intellect, impresses its thoughts and ideas upon it which are the expression of the belief. Thus the creation of the subconscious self is the manifestation of our beliefs.

The primary aim of healing is to change the wrong consciousness and beliefs. Very frequently the wrong state of consciousness which externalises as illness or disease is the mistaken idea that some secondary cause which is really only a condition is the primary cause.

In reality there is only one primary cause for such phenomena, viz., the subjective or subconscious mind. The subconscious mind is so primitive, basic, and elemental, with roots so deep in our being that its power is difficult to comprehend. It belongs to the plane of the absolute, it functions without the limitations of time and space whereas the conscious mind or intellect perceives things in the limited aspect of form and time and space.

If you ever conceive of yourself in the absolute or unconditioned the conception that arises is that of pure living spirit, unhampered by conditions of any kind and therefore not subject to illness. This mental concept must be impressed upon the subconscious mind of the patient being treated and it will become externalised.

It is not always easy to apply this principle in practice because most people have held all their lives the false belief that disease is a substantial entity, a reality in itself, and is of course looked upon as a primary cause instead of as a merely negative condition resulting from the *absence* of a primary cause. It is a common occurrence in healing that after a definite improvement in the patient's health has become apparent the old symptoms reappear. This is because the new belief in his own creative faculty and in the power of Colour has not fully penetrated into the subconscious. Each succeeding treatment and each application of Colour-rays helps the subconscious mind to build up the right attitude until finally the permanent cure is effected.

In the mental aspect of healing the Healer substitutes his own conscious mind and will for that of the patient in order to reach the patient's subconscious mind and to impress upon it the conception of perfect health. The Healer likewise impresses upon the subconscious mind of the patient certain colours which he knows will give the right healing vibration.

A question that will be asked is—" How can the Healer substitute his own conscious mind for that of the patient ? " The patient is asked to put himself in a receptive mental attitude which is not the same thing as blanking out his mind or surrendering his will. He is asked to exercise his will so as to remove the barrier of his own objective personality and to open his mind to the thought-force of the Healer. The Healer adopts the same attitude but in a reverse manner : while the patient lays aside the personality barrier with the object of allowing the power to flow in, the Healer does so with the object of allowing the power to flow out.

True healing is a partnership between healer and

patient. The mutual removal of the personality barrier results in the condition known as contact or *rapport*—the cosmic forces will then be polarised according to the universal law of Nature. The finer forces of light and colour operate best when harmony exists. When the personality barriers which are similar to the language barriers between persons of different nationality have been removed, the Healer can address the subconscious self of the patient as though it were his own. If we concentrate the mind on the diseased condition of the patient we are conscious of him as a separate personality which is the antithesis of sure spirit. The right attitude is the conception of him as a ray of pure spirit which enables us to contact his innermost being.

The Colour healer withdraws his thought from the contemplation of symptoms and from the physical-personality aspect and thinks of him as a spiritual being composed of pure light, not subject to any conditions and able to externalise all the spiritual qualities inherent within.

With this concept firmly held in his mind the Healer can then make mental affirmations that he shall build up in the physical and etheric bodies the correspondence of that spiritual vitality which exists deep within. This thought-form is moulded by the Healer's conscious mind at the same time that the patient's conscious mind is accepting or believing the fact that he is receiving the thought-stream of the Healer. As a result of this mental process the patient's subconscious mind becomes firmly impressed with the recognition of its own vital and health-giving power. The subconscious mind aided by the restorative vibrations of Colour carries into outward manifestation the picture impressed upon it : the negative condition of illness then gives way to new health.

It will be seen in the above statement that no attempt is made to dominate or hypnotise the patient's mind. The aim is to arouse and strengthen the patient's own resources by a partnership of harmony and co-operation. To achieve this mental partnership it is very necessary to instruct the patient in the broad principles of spiritual Colour-healing. Sometimes, however, this may not be possible or advisable. Patients may have deeply-rooted prejudices, scepticism, resentment or extreme detachment which make conscious and voluntary *rapport* impossible. The alternative method, that of Absent healing, may then be applied.

Since the healing rays are universal and omnipresent and the subconscious mind or the higher consciousness is not limited in its power of action to the senses or the dimension of time and space it is therefore quite immaterial whether the patient be in the immediate presence of the Healer or in a distant country.

The essence of Absent Colour Treatments is the holding in the mind a Colour that is required for healing the sufferer. At some previously agreed-on time the Healer should enter his Sanctuary of Colour or take his place before a Colour Shrine or Altar dedicated to the transmission of the Rays and then tune-in mentally with the correct Colour Ray. He should hold the letter of the patient and impress upon his mind the name and address : this should be repeated several times. He then reviews rapidly in his mind the symptoms or the disease to be treated and afterwards concentrates on the following (or some similar) formula. " I project to so-and-so the Orange Ray of vitality and restoration and call upon the Cosmic Power to aid me in this work of restoring health and harmony to his system. Through the White Light of Spirit I call forth the latent powers within his being to cast out the negative conditions of disease. I direct the Cosmic Healing Rays to replenish his aura and remove all roots and causes of his disease." He repeats the patient's name again and at the same time radiates from his aura whatever colours he desires to send out.

It is not necessary to devote any great length of time to each individual patient : from three to five minutes expended on each is usually sufficient. The patient for his part should remain passive and receptive for about one hour so that his depleted system may fully absorb the cosmic healing vibrations.

Although this Colour Treatment is purely on the mental-spiritual plane it is helpful in some cases to turn on a Colour-lamp during the treatment period. This uplifts the physical vibrations and creates a fitting atmosphere. The patient should be advised as to the time of the treatment and should be asked to hold himself in a relaxed and receptive state of mind. This is not to say that healers cannot do good to sufferers without their knowledge— this is being done every day. The Healing Rays are well able to benefit a patient without his knowledge or expectation just as a thought can be impressed on the minds of most people at any time by telepathy. But it is found in practice that the conscious co-operation of healer and patient is the best arrangement in Absent Treatments.

A word may here be said about the value of sending healing vibrations at night. If you are in pain or trouble yourself, such a thought-radiation sent to a friend will lighten your pain or worry : if you are sleepless, it will swiftly tranquillise your mind, restoring the nerve-balance and flooding your system with harmony : if you awake during the night you will quickly regain rest by recalling the suffering of some patient and sending out a healing vibration.

An important link between healer and patient is the writing of letters. A letter conveys far more than the written sentences it contains—it carries the vital magnetism and radiations of the writer including the thought-aura. The patient should be encouraged to write periodically concerning his health condition and the Healer should answer his promptly. A personal letter, not a duplicated circular, should always be sent.

Finally, the student of Colour-healing should bear in mind the words of a great spiritual Master : " A mental Colour Treatment is an activity of great beauty and power in the higher planes and is of great benefit and refreshment to the Healer as well as to the patient."

THE POWER OF THE RAYS

The Science of Colour-Healing

By S. G. J. OUSELEY

CONTENTS

THE SCIENCE OF THE AURA

A Practical Guide to the Study of the Human Aura

By S. G. J. OUSELEY